The book talks directly and engagingly about the way storytelling can profoundly affect someone's life from first tentative encounter to a glorious and joyful tool and metaphor for life and work.
Michael Harvey, Storyteller

Our own life story - as presented to ourselves and the world around us - is a powerful and transformatory device. The power of Coming Home to Story lies in Mead's passion and adventure, his faith in stories and storytelling as a source of creativity, healing and sustenance. It is the story as a means of confronting fears, doubts and threats and, as he writes in the prologue, how stories "deepen and perhaps even transform what is possible".
Bristol Review of Books

The art and craft of storytelling from the inside out. The reader is taken on a fascinating and visceral journey into the heart of storytelling, living alongside the author as he falls in love with his new calling, wrestling inner and outer demons along the way. If you are even remotely interested in the power of story to transform your life, read this book.
Richard Olivier, founding voice within Mythodrama and Artistic Director of Olivier Mythodrama

Geoff Mead does a lovely job of enchanting the world, of breathing a touch of magic into our daily existence. The book tells the story of his own journey into becoming a storyteller, and adds the delightful spice of some of his own favourite stories. What you get is an extremely accessible account of the challenges and promises of this art form.
Omair Ahmad, Author of The Storyteller's Tale

If you didn't believe before that the storyteller can be both healer and magician, you could hardly not believe it after reading this book. I feel the better, and the wiser, for having read this inspiring text.
Fact and Fiction Magazine

This wonderful and illuminating book takes the reader inside the experience of telling and listening to stories. The book itself tells a story: the author's own personal odyssey to become a whole person as he engages with the challenges of becoming a professional storyteller. He weaves in some of his most beautiful wonder tales as examples of how stories can enlarge our lives. Geoff shows how stories can take us beyond "happily ever after", into a world of adventure and passion, imagination and heart, in which the listener and teller can participate in the whole of existence.
Judith Hemming, Founder, Moving Constellations

I read this book in one long refreshing draught before the sun came up on a brand new day and I am delighted to say that the Muse has not deserted Geoff. Wasting no time, he plunges us straight into an inspiring, intriguing and important exploration about our relationship with story which has immediate relevance for those of us working with or interested in the role of story and narrative today. Written with an insight, rigour and vulnerability that moved me on many levels, I can heartily recommend this book to anyone who senses the possibility of a deeper connection with the story world of imagination and meaning.
Sue Hollingsworth, Co-Director, International School of Storytelling

Coming Home to Story
Storytelling Beyond Happily Ever After

Geoff Mead

For Kathryn

To be human is to tell stories

Geoff Mead

Dec 2013

◣◢ Vala

First published in 2011 by Vala Publishing Co-operative
Paperback edition published in 2013
Copyright © Geoff Mead
Vala Publishing Co-operative Ltd
8 Gladstone Street, Bristol, BS3 3AY, UK
For further information on Vala publications, see
www.valapublishers.coop or write to info@valapublishers.coop

Cover design, illustrations and typography by Chris Seeley

Typeset in Freya, designed by Saku Heinänen
Printed and bound by CPI Group (UK) Ltd, Croydon, CR0 4YY

The paper used is Munken Premium, which is FSC certified.

Storywater by Rumi is reprinted with the kind permission of
Coleman Barks.

The publishers have made every effort to ensure all copyright
holders are acknowledged, but if they have inadvertently overlooked
any, they will be pleased to acknowledge them at the first
opportunity.

A CIP catalogue record for this title is available from
the British Library.
ISBN 978-1-908363-01-5

Dedication

This book is dedicated to the stories my children's children will one day tell their children. And to the memory of my father Raymond Geoffrey Mead and mother Vera Grace King whose long-ago love story made all these stories possible.

Contents

Prologue: Swimming in the Sea of Stories   3

Section 1: Being & Becoming a Storyteller
Chapter 1: Falling in Love with Story   13
Story 1: The Banyan Deer   20
Chapter 2: Joining the Company of Storytellers   25
Chapter 3: Master & Servant   37
Chapter 4: A Moment of Grace   42
Story 2: Jumping Mouse   49

Section 2: Healing Fictions
Chapter 5: In Bed with the Bear   61
Chapter 6: Stories all the Way Down   69
Chapter 7: Storied Lives   77
Chapter 8: Living Stories   84
Story 3: The Giant with No Heart in His Body   91
Chapter 9: Telling the Untold Story   100
Chapter 10: Hermes in the Gorge   106

Section 3: Men & Storytelling
Chapter 11: We Band of Brothers   117
Story 4: The Furthest Shore   128
Chapter 12: Fathers & Sons   142
Chapter 13: Sons & Fathers   149

Section 4: Widening Circles
Chapter 14: Some Enchanted Evening   161
Story 5: The Magic Garden of the Poor   170
Chapter 15: Storytelling in Organisations   177
Chapter 16: Water on the Rock   187

Epilogue: Coming Home to Story   199

Frontispiece

The old storytellers were the first real explorers and frontierspeople of the abyss. They brought the world within our souls. They made living within and without as one....
And I think now, in our age, in the mid-ocean of our days, with certainties collapsing about us and with the dark descending nights ahead - I think that now we need those fictional old bards and fearless storytellers, those seers.
We need their magic, their courage, their love and their fire more than ever before. It is precisely in a fractured, broken age that we need mystery and a reawakened sense of wonder.
We need them in order to be whole again. We need to be reminded of the primeval terror again. We need to be humble again.
We need to go down to the bottom, to the depths of the heart and start to live all over again as we have never lived before.

A Way of Being Free, Ben Okri

Prologue
Swimming in the Sea of Stories

Like the proverbial fish that cannot see the water they swim in,
we do not notice the medium we dwell within. Unaware that
our stories are stories, we experience them as the world.

David Loy

Prologue
Swimming in the Sea of Stories

We humans are storytelling creatures. We spend most of our waking lives exchanging stories and anecdotes - at home, at work, at play. Telling stories is the primary way we make sense of our experience and give significance to our lives. Children's fables and fairy stories that end "happily ever after" may represent a popular conception of storytelling but they are only one facet of a universal human phenomenon.

Storytelling is enjoying a tremendous renaissance in many fields: entertainment, personal therapy, academic inquiry, business coaching and leadership development to name but a few. Books that theorise about story are plentiful, books that offer storytelling tips and techniques are relatively common but little if anything has been written that takes the reader *inside* the experience of telling and listening to stories.

Coming Home to Story explores the territory beyond "happily ever after", drawing on my own experiences of being and becoming a professional adult storyteller to show (as well as tell) you how stories and storytelling can engage our imaginations, heal our wounded souls, bring people together in community, enable us to make sense of the world around us, and bring adventure and passion into our lives.

These may sound like rather grand claims. The most I can hope to do is to shed a little light on these areas by holding up the lantern of what I have learned during the past decade and a half as I have mastered the practicalities, stumbled into the pitfalls and reached for the potential of storytelling to take us into other worlds so that we may experience our own more deeply. *Coming Home to Story* both tells the story and offers the fruits of that personal odyssey. It is for anyone who has ever listened to or told a story (or wanted to) and anyone who has ever found and followed their calling or who, like me, has waited a long time to discover what it is.

For most of my first five decades, I had a nagging sense that I was living somebody else's life - a life that did not belong to me. As an adult, I was apparently successful in my chosen career (working my way up through the ranks of the police service to become a chief superintendent) with a PhD and a thriving sideline as a part-time academic and consultant. None of these superficial achievements brought much joy and I had little sense of them serving a deeper purpose. At fifty, it seemed either that I had missed my calling or that I was destined not to have one.

I was wrong. The call came late but when it did come it was loud and clear. It turns out that my calling was - and is - to be a storyteller. After several years during which my passion for stories and storytelling had steadily grown, the realisation that storytelling would become my profession came suddenly and dramatically. Afterwards I could no longer resist the siren call of my vocation.

It is 8.00 a.m. Thursday 4th August 2005 and I am sitting on a hard wooden chair in the Speech and Drama Hut (or Screech and Trauma Hut as it is sometimes affectionately known) at Emerson College. Eight or nine other people are similarly seated on chairs scattered randomly around the room.

"The dream matrix is open," says Ashley.

Twelve of us, all storytellers trained at Emerson, have assembled for a weeklong reunion. We have been learning about the Greek muses and I am feeling despondent: how well have I been entertaining the muse? Will she keep calling if I go on ignoring her knock at the door?

In the three years since I finished the Craft of the Storyteller course (a gift I gave myself as part of a six month sabbatical when I retired from the police service) I have been busy earning a living, developing a small consultancy practice, doing far too much routine administration and far too little creative work of any kind.

"I had a dream last night," I say. "I was walking through a city with many tall buildings. None of them were finished and most still had cranes on top. There was no sign of any work being done or other people. In my dream I realised that I was the builder and it was depressing to see so many edifices not brought to completion. Then I felt the ground shake and rumble and suddenly a waterspout, like a dozen express trains strapped together, burst out through the top of one of the buildings and shot up into the sky before the water returned to earth in a huge fountain. The ground carried on shaking and the buildings began to crumble and fall. Floodwaters rose up and swept through the streets. I could only move in one direction - with the water."

We have gathered to share dreams and dream fragments from the night before. We do not comment on the dreams, just speak them out if we are moved to do so and listen silently to others. Sometimes the dreams feel significant, sometimes not. This one stays with me and I reflect on it during the day.

Something has to change. It is quite clear to me that the muse (often associated with wells and springs) is calling me to commit to my own creative impulse and immerse myself in story. What I have done so far is all well and good but I am coming up to 56 years old and what do I have to show for my life but a city of half-completed buildings. I know that storytelling is my passion and my gift. The question is what am I going to do about it? I resolve that evening that I will change the pattern of my work and of my life. The next day as the course closes I declare to the group that I am going to dedicate myself to story and storytelling in all that I do and that somehow I will create the conditions that enable me to live my dream.

The trouble was that I wasn't sure what I needed to do. Life carried on much the same for a few months. Then in December my partner took me to Mousehole in Cornwall for a surprise birthday treat. She bought me a copy of The Mousehole Cat[1] and I read it aloud to her. At the end of the story, when old Tom the fisherman and Mowzer his cat escaped the storm to find the whole village alight with candles and lanterns to bring them safely home, my voice broke and I wept.

As they came in sight of home, a strange sight met their eyes. The whole village of Mousehole was shining with light and lanterns gleamed along both arms of the harbour. For when the people of Mousehole had woken to find old Tom's boat missing and a light left in his window, they knew that he had gone to find fish for them, or to perish on the deep water. All day they had watched and waited, staring out into the cloud-wracked sea, but they could see no sign of him. And when night fell, all the women went home and set candles in all their windows and every man lit his lantern and went down to the harbour walls.

How much I wanted to come home to my self, to be the person I was meant to be; how much I longed to be welcomed for who I was and not who others wanted me to be in the world.

I was born in Redruth but hadn't been to Cornwall for many years. We spent a few days travelling around, discovering the places where I lived for the first two years of my life. The Cornish towns and villages were interesting enough but it was the sea, the sea that called me home. I remembered how much I loved being near water, whether sailing on the sea or fishing on a riverbank. I remembered my dream from the summer and I knew that somehow it was all connected.

I decided that my first step would be to find somewhere to live in sight of the sea. Much of my life had been arid and I needed more water, more juice. I needed to create somewhere beautiful and inspiring to entertain the muse. This couldn't be the office where necessary mundane things get done. It had to have a sacred quality, one that honoured the creative impulse and fed it with solitude and beauty - a garden of the soul, if you like.

I began to look and after a few false starts - the top floor of a fish packing factory in Newlyn, an ornate sandcastle of a building in Seaton, and a shabby warehouse conversion in Bridport - found it two months later in Lyme Regis. It turned out to be a ground floor flat in a Georgian house with French windows onto the lawn looking out over the town to the sea and the great sweep of Lyme Bay, stretching as far as the eye can see, to Chesil Beach and Portland Bill. As soon as I walked in the door, I knew it was the perfect place.

Sun is streaming in through the open windows as I sit writing this at the kitchen table. Gulls are wheeling and screeching overhead and songbirds call to each other in the beech tree at the end of the garden. Here there are no unwanted intrusions, no television and no clutter. Here I keep a few carefully selected books, paintings and keepsakes from my travels, comfortable and well-designed furniture, reasonable wine, copious tea and coffee, and good food. Here is where I feel most at home, where friends occasionally visit, where I think and write, where I go for long walks, where I soak in the bath, where I research and learn new stories.

It is now 2010, a decade and a half since I first encountered storytelling and five years since the dream at Emerson. The pattern of my work and life has changed enormously. Creative projects abound: writing, collecting stories for performances, running workshops on story and storytelling for men, teaching and performing in the UK, Spain, Canada and Japan, taking storytelling into business and government organizations, and setting up a Centre for Narrative Leadership. Living and working in sight of the expansive and ever-changing sea, I feel as though I have found a place in the world where I belong and where I can be myself.

Opening up the space for that wellspring of story to flow has been a huge challenge. I had to let go of some familiar and well-paid work, to spend my life savings, and to trust that working with story would provide a sufficient income. I still have moments of doubt, of wondering whether I am good enough or (worse still) whether I deserve to be doing what I love but I would never go back to how things were. I know with a deep sense of certainty that now, at long last, I have found my vocation. I know that, whatever else happens or does not happen, in the words of Dawna Markova's famous poem, "I will not die an unlived life."

I want to share some of what I have learned and experienced thus far on the journey. I'd like to show you how I came to understand the intrinsic value of stories (and therefore of storytelling): how they help us attribute meaning and significance to our own lives; how they help us make sense of the world; how they help us to understand who we are as individuals and as communities. I want to show you how I learned that stories have enormous power to liberate and transform lives (as well as to oppress and constrain them), starting with my own.

The stories around us and the stories within us are legion. We are swimming in a sea of stories. As a storyteller, I had to learn how stories work, not just at the level of entertainment, but also at a deeper, soul level. Then, and only then, could I use story to begin to heal myself and offer healing to others, and to understand the value of what I had to offer to the leaders and potential leaders of our society, from the chief executives and senior civil servants who control so much of our fate to the educators and social activists who seek to influence those in power. In so doing, I believe I can encourage a more inclusive and more generative view of what is desirable and possible in today's world. That is the real work of a modern-day storyteller; what could be more exciting, challenging or worthwhile?

But this is also an inner journey. Storytelling is not something you can do to people or at people. It can only be done with people. There is an old joke about the difference between involvement and commitment. In a meal of eggs and bacon, the chicken is involved but the pig is committed. In a similar way, I've had to commit myself to my stories and to my craft. As I discovered early on, it is not enough to lay a story before (or even on) an audience, a storyteller has to be willing to be vulnerable, to be prepared to give something of themselves and this sometimes means digging deep into soul territory.

At times the journey has been joyful and touched by grace. At times it has meant painfully letting go of what propped up and sustained me, like the reluctant Lindworm shedding its seven skins to expose the tender flesh beneath. In coming home to story, I found the chance to come home to myself, closer to my real and better self, closer to living the life I came here for.

Ultimately, that is what the book you now hold in your hands is about: the transformative and soulful journey of being and becoming a storyteller, such that I now live "labouring in ecstasy", as the poet Yeats puts it, using stories to deepen and perhaps even transform what is possible around me, at the same time as they help me to heal myself. It is a path open to anyone willing to let stories into their souls and put them back out into the world.

Being & Becoming a Storyteller

The art of storytelling lies within the storyteller,
to be searched for, drawn out, made to grow.

Ruth Sawyer

1
Falling in Love with Story

The first thing any budding storyteller has to do is find the place within them that loves stories, particularly the place that loves listening to stories. All the good storytellers that I know relish well-told tales and are willing to travel far and wide to seek them out. Something magical happens when you sit down and really *listen* to a story unfolding. I stress the word listen because I am not talking about reading a story from a book or watching a story at the theatre, or on film or television. Even stories on radio, gripping though they can be, tend to be tightly scripted and lack the immediacy and intimacy of live storytelling.

When a storyteller who knows their craft stands up in front of an audience and tells a story (whether contemporary or traditional, real-life or imagined, spontaneous or rehearsed) it emerges in the space between teller and listener. The storyteller's words are evanescent. The story moves on, leaving listeners to discover each twist and turn of the plot as it unfolds. They cannot rewind or fast-forward the film; they cannot flick through the pages of the book to check what has happened or to anticipate the ending. Instead, the listener's attention is held (or not) moment by moment in the ever-moving present. Each telling and listening is unique. Emotions arise and subside, images come and go as each listener feels the story running through their body and co-creates the story with the storyteller in their own imagination. The Sufi poet Rumi[2] put this wonderfully in his poem *Storywater:*

A story is like the water
that heats your bath.
It takes messages between the fire
and your skin. It lets them meet,
and it cleans you!

Very few can sit down
in the middle of the fire itself
like a salamander or Abraham.
We need intermediaries.

A feeling of fullness comes,
but usually it take some bread
to bring it.

Beauty surrounds us,
but usually we need to be walking
in a garden to know it.

The body itself is a screen
to shield and partially reveal
the light that's blazing
inside your presence.

Water, stories, the body,
all the things we do, are mediums
that hide and show what's hidden.

Study them,
and enjoy this being washed
with a secret we sometimes know,
and then not.

I love the idea of stories washing over and through us; we are indeed swimming in a sea of stories. Of course, stories can be told badly with too little detail or too much, in a monotone or mumbled, in a rambling or tendentious manner, or to serve the storyteller's ego rather than the needs and desires of the audience. Storytellers owe it to themselves and to their listeners (and indeed to the stories) to learn their craft and tell their stories well. Rumi's *Storywater* should be regarded as an aspiration not an assumption. In our post-oral, literate, textual and digital age, the art of storytelling has to be re-learned. The magic that we long for as tellers and listeners does not necessarily come easily and, as I began this chapter by saying, there is no better way to begin learning and understanding the craft of the storyteller than by listening.

Thanks to the revival in oral storytelling that has taken place in the United Kingdom over the past few decades, there are many opportunities to experience high quality storytelling. Clubs, festivals and even small theatres promote storytelling events. My own introduction to the world of storytelling came unexpectedly (and unlooked-for) at a conference on complexity theory and organisational development in 1996 when, against my better judgement if not actually against my will, I joined thirty or forty other conference delegates in the lounge area at Roffey Park Management Centre for an evening performance by a couple of professional storytellers.

All the chairs and sofas were occupied. There were cushions scattered on the floor with people sitting and lying on them too. I squeezed myself in and sat down as best as I could on half a cushion. The laughing, chattering voices in the room quietened to a whisper and all eyes focused on two men perched on stools at the far end of the room. One of them was tall, with wild, bushy, grey hair. He was forty-something and wearing a brightly-coloured waistcoat. "Old hippy," I thought to myself. The other man was smaller, slighter with white crew-cut hair, a bit younger, I guessed. He had a distinctive lopsided smile and bright eyes. My friend Paul Roberts who had organised the conference stood up, introduced them as Ashley Ramsden and Bernard Kelly, then sat down again.

Ashley and Bernard looked around the room catching our eyes and we hushed. After a few moments of silence, Bernard took an audible breath, leaned forward and began to speak.

Once, near the holy city of Benares, the Buddha reincarnated in the form of a Banyan deer. Even as a fawn his appearance was marvellous: his coat shone with a soft golden hue, his eyes sparkled like diamonds, the horns that were to grow into many-pointed antlers were silver, his hooves gleamed like black jet and struck showers of sparks from the ground when he pranced. The years passed and he grew into a magnificent stag - the king of the Banyan deer - and he led his herd wisely and well. Then one day, in the world of men, a new king came to power, a young man in the flower of his youth. His name was Brahmadatta and he loved nothing so much as hunting.

"Oh dear," I thought. "It's that kind of story." There was a slight pause and I sneaked a glance at my neighbours in the audience to see what they were making of it. They were still and attentive. They seemed to be enjoying it, although it occurred to me that perhaps they were just being polite. I returned my gaze to the storyteller and then, despite my scepticism, I began to wonder how the fates of the king of men and the king of the banyan deer would cross, as they surely must.

The king and his retinue rampaged through the countryside trapping and shooting every creature that came into their view. Each evening they returned to court followed by wagons piled high with the spoils of the hunt: carcasses of bear, leopard, tiger, monkey, boar, buffalo and deer.

And I realised that I could see them all: the antlered banyan deer, the proud young king with bow and arrow on horseback, the courtiers doing their best to keep up, the wagons and carts overflowing with death. I could smell the blood, feel the panic of the startled and terrified animals. My body was sitting on the same cushion in the same room but my imagination had taken flight. I'd been transported to that other world in no more time than it has taken me to write the opening words of the story.

*The king of the Banyan deer took his herd deeper and deeper
into the forest to escape the slaughter. Meanwhile the people
began to demand that something had to be done to stop the king's
huntsmen from trampling the grain, scaring the cattle and laying
waste to the land. Things got so bad that crops were not harvested
and taxes were not paid. In the face of such strong protests,
Brahmadatta reluctantly agreed to curtail his activities: instead of
roaming freely, a certain area would be set aside for him to hunt. A
portion of woodland was fenced and the king's men beat the trees
with clubs and yelled at the top of their voices to drive the denizens
of the forest into the killing field.*

Another pause and I noticed the effect the story was having
on my body. My gaze was soft, my mouth open and jaw slack,
breath deep and slow. I took another quick peek at others in
the audience. It was the same everywhere I looked. We had
all been caught. The story resumed and I listened to the easy
flow of words, relishing the images that welled up inside me,
thrilled by the magic that had brought us so quickly to a sense
of communion with something ancient and timeless. My
heart thumped with excitement. What was going on?

I have thought about that first encounter with storytelling
many times since then, trying to understand better how
listening to stories can stir our imaginations, touch our hearts,
and bring a group of people together. The readiness and
openness of the listener is an obvious factor: listeners must
consent to listen otherwise the story comes as an imposition.
In this case, the advertising of the event and the arrangement
of the room created a tacit contract between tellers and
listeners: we had agreed to our respective roles (although our
consent to listen was conditional upon the assumption that
the storytellers would engage us with their stories). We were
ready and willing to bathe in "Story Water".

But that just created a space of possibility. The magic arrived
in the form of words that created rich and vibrant images,
words that triggered our imaginations to be able to see, hear,
touch, smell and taste the invisible world of the story. James
Hillman, who extended the work of Carl Gustav Jung in the

field of archetypal psychology, puts it this way:

> *Word-images... are [the] immediate property of imagination ... they are free from the perceptible world and free one from it. They take the mind home to its poetic base, to the imaginal.* [3]

And what might explain the way in which the audience that evening came together? Our individual imaginations may have been stirred and our hearts touched by the characters in the story and their fates, but what caused the quality of relationships between us to shift? We were all experiencing the same story, hearing the same words at the same time although our sympathies may have differed greatly. We were all spellbound by the same magic and that clearly had something to do with it.

Eventually, I found a more profound explanation in the work of Walter Ong who in his classic study of the development of language and literacy[4] recalls the power of the spoken word for our pre-literate ancestors (and indeed for us when we experience it):

> *Because in its physical constitution as sound, the spoken word proceeds from the human interior and manifests human beings to one another as conscious interiors, as persons, the spoken word forms human beings into close-knit groups. When a speaker is addressing an audience, the members of the audience normally become a unity, with themselves and with the speaker.*

At the physiological level, because the spoken word is sounded, we literally vibrate or resonate at the same frequency through the complex and delicate mechanism of the inner ear. We are, so to speak, on the same wavelength. It has always been this way, so it should not surprise us that storytelling often evokes an ancient folk-memory as if sitting round a fire, listening to tribal elders or travelling bards.

Fascinating as these explanations are, I would not want

to reduce the experience of storytelling to simple cause and effect. Mystery and wonder lie at the heart of magic and the storyteller is a kind of magician, summoning up whole worlds, making the invisible appear, bringing the story to life so that though we may not believe it, we believe *in* it. That evening at Roffey Park, we were in the hands of master magicians, storytellers at the height of their powers. Although I did not know it beforehand, at some level I must have been ready because, in an uncharacteristic *coup de foudre*, there and then I fell in love with story.

Ashley and Bernard told many stories that evening. We travelled together through time and across continents with tales of kings and queens, fishermen and fairies, saints and sinners. I didn't want the evening to finish - though of course it had to and did, all too soon. As we applauded and Ashley and Bernard took a final bow I could not wait any longer. I rushed over to them, oblivious of anyone else in the room. "How do you learn to do this? I have to learn to how to do this." I was almost incoherent with excitement. "I have to learn how to tell stories."

I was lucky. I wonder what would have happened if I'd had a bad experience, if instead of the wonderful Ashley and Bernard there had been a couple of dreadful ranters or a pair of awkward mumblers or a brace of mannered, clichéd, are-you-sitting-comfortably s-t-o-r-y-t-e-l-l-e-r-s of the kind that make one wince and squirm with embarrassment. Had that been the case, I may never have given storytelling a second chance.

I was doubly lucky. When I blurted out my enthusiastic desire to learn how to tell stories, Ashley laughed and told me that he ran a school for storytelling. "It's not far from here, at Emerson College. You'd better start coming along." Within a week I'd signed up for my first storytelling course. Sometimes, when the right thing or the right person comes along, everything falls into place and all you have to do is say, "Yes!"

The Banyan Deer

Once, near the holy city of Benares, the Buddha reincarnated in the form of a Banyan deer. Even as a fawn his appearance was marvellous: his coat shone with a soft golden hue, his eyes sparkled like diamonds, the horns that were to grow into many-pointed antlers were silver, his hooves gleamed like black jet and struck showers of sparks from the ground when he pranced. The years passed and he grew into a magnificent stag - the king of the Banyan deer - and he led his herd wisely and well.

Then one day, in the world of men, a new king came to power, a young man in the flower of his youth. His name was Brahmadatta and he loved nothing so much as hunting. The king and his retinue rampaged through the countryside trapping and shooting every creature that came into their view. Each evening they returned to court followed by wagons piled high with the spoils of the hunt: carcasses of bear, leopard, tiger, monkey, boar, buffalo and deer.

The king of the Banyan deer took his herd deeper and deeper into the forest to escape the slaughter. Meanwhile the people began to demand that something had to be done to stop the king's huntsmen from trampling the grain, scaring the cattle and laying waste to the land. Things got so bad that crops were not harvested and taxes were not paid. In the face of such strong protests, Brahmadatta reluctantly agreed to curtail his activities: instead of roaming freely, a certain area would be set aside for him to hunt. A portion of woodland was fenced and the king's men beat the trees with clubs and yelled at the top of their voices to drive the denizens of the forest into the killing field. The largest of the creatures trapped in this way were the Banyan deer and another herd, the Branch deer.

A wooden tower was built by the fence, a vantage point from which the royal huntsmen could shoot their metal-tipped arrows into the milling herds of deer. Brahmadatta looked down and for the first time saw the kings of the Banyan deer and the Branch deer. He had never seen such magnificent animals. "These two must be spared. No one is to shoot them," he decreed.

Each day the huntsmen came and the carnage was terrible. Deer were killed and wounded indiscriminately, they even injured each other in their panic to escape the death raining down on them. Although he was untouched by the arrows, the king of the Banyan deer was deeply distressed by the suffering he saw all around him. "Friend," he told the king of the Branch deer, "Many deer are perishing. Perhaps we cannot prevent the king from taking their lives but we can at least stop the others being wounded. Instead of all trying to flee the arrows, let one deer agree to stand before the archers each day. Let us draw lots for this. The turn shall fall one day on my herd and the next on yours. It is a terrible solution but better than what is happening now."

The king of the Branch deer agreed. The next day, lots were drawn and a single deer stood trembling in front of the tower to be killed. Brahmadatta could see what was happening and was moved. "These deer kings are wise," he told his followers. "They have decided to offer a single life rather than let all suffer from our hunt. Such a noble sacrifice demands respect. Shoot only the deer that stands before us." But it was poor sport and beneath the dignity of a king. Brahmadatta put down his bow unused and returned to the palace leaving his huntsmen to provide the venison for his table.

Things went on like this for some time until one day the lot was drawn by a pregnant doe of the Branch herd. She went to speak to her king. "I will willingly take my turn when my fawn has come into the world but for the sake of the life that is within me, let me be spared this day." But the king of the Branch deer replied "There can be no exceptions. You have drawn the lot and therefore you must die. No-one is above the law. If you refuse there will be no place for you among the deer of my herd."

Desperate, the doe ran to find the king of the Banyan deer. She bowed her head low and begged for his assistance. He listened quietly to her plea then gave his answer. "The terms of the lottery require one life to be taken, not two. You shall not die this day. You are free to go." Shaking with relief, the doe pledged her allegiance and that of her unborn fawn to their new king for as long as they both should live. "But who will take our place?" she asked.

"Leave the matter to me, I shall see to it," said the king of the Banyan deer, turning to leave. He looked round at the deer of the Banyan herd and the Branch herd, browsing peacefully in the early morning light. He had spared the doe's life and he was not willing to lay the burden upon another. It was his to bear. He walked calmly towards the fence and stood in front of the archers on the wooden tower, the sun glinting on his silver antlers, his coat shining with a soft golden hue. He did not shake or tremble with fear but stood tall and proud, piercing them with his brilliant, diamond-like eyes.

The huntsmen saw at once that this was no ordinary deer to be culled for the pot but one of those that Brahmadatta himself had decreed should be spared. They were in a quandary, knowing that they must not shoot the stag but fearing to return empty-handed. They sent a messenger to the palace asking the king to come at once. Brahmadatta rode swiftly to the palisade, dismounted and climbed the wooden tower alone to face the stag. They looked at each other for a long moment, one king to another.

"Don't you know that you are spared from the hunt," said Brahmadatta. "Why are you standing here in front of my archers?"

"This morning, a pregnant doe asked for my help. She pledged allegiance to me as her king. The lottery requires that one life be taken, not two. I would not place her burden upon another. I have come to take her place."

Brahmadatta pondered these words and gazed in wonder at the majestic creature in front of him. His face flushed with shame and admiration. "Noble deer, your action is indeed worthy of a monarch. You have taught me a valuable lesson, one I shall not forget: it is our duty as kings to care for all our subjects, even the least among them. In recompense, I grant you and all your herd freedom from my hunt. Go free and live well."

The king of the Banyan deer did not move. "Thank you Sire for your gift but I cannot accept it. If you spare me and all the Banyan deer then your men will simply slaughter the Branch deer in our place. Their suffering would not be less than ours. I would not buy our freedom at such a price."

"You would risk your life and the lives of your herd to save the Branch deer?" asked Brahmadatta. "This is beyond a king's duty, even one as wise and courageous as you."

"Picture the rain of death and suffering that would fall on them in our place. Think, O king of men, and let them also go free."

Brahmadatta bowed his head, realising that he had met his match in nobility and compassion. "Very well. How can I deny you? They too shall be spared. Now will you go in peace?"

"How can I go in peace, your Majesty, knowing that, although we deer are free, the bear, the leopard, the tiger, the monkey, the boar, the buffalo and the other creatures of the earth will daily risk death at the hands of you and your huntsmen? How could there be peace for us if not for them also? I would not buy our freedom at such a price."

Brahmadatta was stunned. Such a thought had never occurred to him. But it was true, he realised. Neither in the realm of animals nor the realm of men could there truly be peace for one if there was not peace for all. His heart opened, tears sprang from his eyes and he stood humbled before the Buddha's reincarnated form. "You are right, great Deer king. No more will they be hunted in my kingdom. I will decree it so. Now will you go, or is there more?"

"Lord Brahmadatta, if only it were that easy. You have spared the creatures of the earth but what of the birds that fly in the air, what of the fish that swim in the water? Would their suffering be any less than ours? Are they not equally deserving of our compassion? How can I walk free knowing that your arrows, nets and hooks lie in wait for them?"

Brahmadatta wept. "Great being," he said, "I have never thought this way before but I can see it now: all are equally deserving and all shall be spared. I will have it proclaimed throughout my land that henceforth no animal, bird or fish is to be hunted, trapped or killed. You have the word of a king that it shall be so. Will you go now, my teacher?"

"Yes," said the king of the Banyan deer. He threw up his head and jumped for joy, high into the air. His silver antlers glittered in the bright noon sun, his coat glowed like burnished gold, and his jet black hooves threw up a shower of sparks when they struck the ground. He fixed Brahmadatta one last time with his diamond-bright eyes. "Yes, now I can go."

The fences that had held the deer trapped were thrown down.

Brahmadatta stayed, watching the herds of Banyan deer and Branch deer go their separate ways, slipping into the shadows, threading their way between the trees, until the last of them had disappeared into the forest. Then, with a new feeling of lightness in his heart, he rode back to the palace.

King Brahmadatta ruled in Benares for many years attaining a great age and a reputation as the wisest and most compassionate of rulers. Towards the end of his days he returned to the forest and erected a stone monument on the very spot where he had once spoken with the Banyan deer. On it were inscribed these words: "Here, taught by the king of deer, Brahmadatta, king of men, learned the true nature of wisdom and compassion."

The king of the Banyan deer also lived to a good age. When it was time for the Buddha to leave that life, his place as ruler of the herd was taken by another – that same fawn whose life he had saved whilst still unborn.

About the story

The origins of this story are very old. It is one of many Indian Buddhist teaching stories known collectively as the *Jataka,* recounting mythical reincarnations of the Buddha. There is a version called *The Banyan-Deer Jataka* in *Stories of the Buddha,* (2005) translated by Caroline Rhys Davids, Pilgrims Publishing, Varanasi, India. The version that I tell (and which appears here) is drawn and adapted from an un-named story in *Soul Food* (1996) edited by Jack Kornfield and Christina Feldman, HarperSanFrancisco, California.

2
Joining the Company of Storytellers

In the process of being and becoming a storyteller, our initial enthusiasm will carry us a good way. We all have some natural capacity to tell a story, we just have to overcome our fear of appearing foolish and give it a go. Most people find they can manage this relatively easily though, of course, there are some budding storytellers for whom learned cultural imperatives or deeply ingrained shyness are significant obstacles to standing up in public. They can take comfort from the knowledge that sensitive folk who find their voices often make better storytellers than those who are more thick-skinned and apparently self-confident.

In any event, let us imagine that somehow, somewhere you have discovered storytelling and that you have already listened to some great storytellers. You felt intrigued by their art and inspired to try your hand; you have begun to tell a few stories yourself though you would not yet put your hand up and claim to be a storyteller. After the first flush of excitement and relief when you managed to get through a whole story without forgetting the plot, you have gradually grown in confidence and you have begun to experience the delight that comes when someone laughs or is moved by your tales. You have taken the first steps but if you carry on telling stories you will inevitably bump up against the limits of your innate competence and native wit.

Instead of feeling justifiably pleased with your modest successes, you begin to see the yawning gulf between your own ability to hold an audience and that of the master storytellers who inspired you in the first place. It seems to happen to everyone on the way to becoming a storyteller. It certainly happened to me. It is a defining moment and our response to it is critical. We can decide that the gap is too big for us to bridge and set our sights lower (or worse still, give up completely) or we can decide to jump right into the gap and look for a good teacher.

There is an old saying that when the pupil is ready the teacher appears and I was lucky enough to find two skilled and generous storytelling teachers: Ashley Ramsden and Sue Hollingsworth from the International School of Storytelling at Emerson College in Forest Row, East Sussex. They still teach there and I would recommend them and their colleagues at the School to anyone wanting to follow the storyteller's path. They held my hand in the very early days as I took my first tentative steps in storytelling and they were on hand to guide me a few years later as I came to the fork in the road and faced that defining moment of choice: to remain as someone who told stories or to commit myself to becoming a storyteller. By that time I had an inkling that I might have the potential to tell a good story but it was only an inkling, a secret desire to perform in public. I had yet to choose or be chosen to join the company of storytellers.

That moment came for me during a weekend storytelling course with Ashley and Sue at Gaunts House in Dorset. There I learned the difference between simply telling a story (objectified as something separate from the teller) and practising the storyteller's art in which story and teller are inseparable (the storyteller bringing himself or herself to the story and finding the resonances of the story in their own life). This was such an important lesson in the dynamics of storytelling and, I am convinced, such an essential requirement of being and becoming a storyteller that it deserves to be told in full.

On the first day of the course, we had been divided into small groups to practise telling a story and get feedback from each other. "Any story will do, maybe one you have heard or read." This simple instruction drove me towards panic. I didn't have a large repertoire of stories to choose from, a couple maybe but they felt a bit tired and old hat. I wanted to work on a fresh story, something with a bit of life in it. I cast around in my mind and what I caught were not stories but vivid recollections of a recent trip I had taken to China. Three months previously I had been part of an official police mission to Yunnan, a remote and rural province struggling to modernise with the first signs of an enterprise culture beginning to emerge.

So many rich and strange images returned as I thought of my visit: fishermen casting their nets from boats on the lakes as they had done for centuries; hundreds of slaughtered ducks hanging by the roadside to cure in the wind; groups of old men and women doing their morning Tai Chi in the parks; our self-confident and energetic host, Superintendent Mah Ji-Yan; Jin-Lian, our shy and pretty interpreter caught blushing and giggling between her desire to appear friendly and her natural modesty.

Surely there was something here to draw upon? I raked my memory but I was sure I didn't know any Chinese stories. Then suddenly I remembered a little Japanese folk tale called *Senjo and Her Soul*[5] that I had come across a few weeks before. I had enjoyed reading it, just half a dozen paragraphs related by Zen master John Daido Loori and I was pretty sure that I could remember the plot. I would transplant the story onto Chinese soil. Maybe I could bring it to life if I allowed it to come through some of the images I had experienced and people I had met in Yunnan.

Stories can be learned word-perfect but they can also happen in the moment. Maybe that is why people sometimes talk about storytellers spinning a yarn or weaving a story. At its best, storytelling is like pulling the strong threads of the narrative through a rich field of imagery, the warp and weft of a bold and colourful tapestry. I knew enough by this time to know that storytelling is more about imagination than memory, more about presence than technique and I decided that when it came to my turn to tell in the small group, I'd try my hand at Senjo.

I was lucky enough to travel to China this summer. I went on an official police mission to Yunnan Province and Beijing. It was a fascinating experience - including singing the Little Green Frog to a hall full of senior police officers and communist party officials - but that is another story! One thing I learned is that Zen koans, you know those little paradoxical questions that they drive themselves crazy with in meditation, are often originally drawn from folk tales and I want to tell you one such tale that I came across and maybe ask ourselves the koan and see if it drives us crazy too.

I had started on familiar territory, setting the scene and claiming (with storyteller's license) some relationship with the story and the right to tell it. Now was the moment to slip into the story itself, to segue from our world into the world of the story. Instinctively I knew that it would not work if I stood outside the story. I had to try and enter that world I told myself, and tell what I see, hear, smell, touch, taste. Trust the story. You know the story. Let it live through you. Here we go.

In Yunnan province, in southwest China, a great river makes its way from the mountains to the sea and along its banks there are many towns and villages. At this time, many years ago, the only means of transport were your own two feet, with pack animals for heavy loads, and boats of various shapes and sizes. Along the river, merchants and tradesmen plied their wares from punts filled with fresh produce: rice, vegetables, flowers, cloth and so forth.

Come with me upstream from the sea, past paddy fields sloshing with newly-planted rice, past fishermen casting their nets, past ramshackle bamboo huts, past forests streaming with morning dew, until we come to Rivertown, three or four days' travel inland.

Ashley slipped quietly into the room and sat down. He had dropped in to listen to our stories and I suddenly felt nervous. I had already set the scene and needed to get on with the story. OK, so what was to happen next?

In a prosperous suburb are the houses of the well-to-do, broad streets lined with desirable residences and standing at the end of one such avenue was a particular house. The sunlight gleamed off the red tiled roof and glinted in the jet-black eyes of the four carved dragons on the eaves, guarding the house against evil spirits. There were children laughing and playing in the garden. Servants clattered through the house, caged birds were singing. The master of the house was a man of middle years, forty perhaps or fifty. It is hard to tell his age.

At last some people. It was time for the characters to appear. I wanted them to be more than cardboard cutouts. I wanted them to be believable, to feel substantial, three-dimensional. I needed to have particular people in mind as I introduced the characters. I thought of the old men and women doing Tai Chi in the park in Kunming City and of Jin-Lian our interpreter and our host Mah Ji-Yan and wondered if they would mind appearing in this story.

If you had looked closely you would have seen deep lines scored round his eyes, lines of grief as well as joy. Grief: because three years previously his wife and elder daughter had died when a plague had swept through the town. Joy: because his younger daughter had survived. She was eight years old and the light of his life, as beautiful as her name Jin-Lian, which means Golden Lotus. At that moment, Jin-Lian was dangling upside-down from the branch of a tree making faces at her best friend and constant companion, ten-year-old Mah Ji-Yan, the son of a poor but respectable clerk.

"Jin-Lian, come down from that tree and stay in the shade. Mah Ji-Yan, you should know better than to lead my daughter astray," her father called.

"Come on, Jin-Lian, we'd better do what your father says".

Jin-Lian dropped like a monkey to the ground. "Can't catch me," she yelled, still pulling faces, and ran into the house.

And so the years passed. Jin-Lian grew into a young woman and Mah Ji-Yan into manhood and the childhood friends became lovers. Secret lovers because in those days fathers chose who their daughters would marry and it was already clear that Jin-Lian's father would not be satisfied with a clerk's son, no matter how honest, industrious or good-looking, no matter - even - how much his daughter loved him.

I paused and looked around the room. I had set the hook. Now we all knew that something was going to happen. We had a story on our hands. Of course, I knew how it was going to end but I was in no hurry and my listeners seemed content for me to let the story unfold at its own pace.

Three months before her sixteenth birthday, Jin-Lian's father summoned her to his room.

"My dearest daughter, you know I want only the best for you. I am happy to tell you that I have found you a fine husband. The son of my oldest friend - he is a good man, kind and gentle, wealthy too. His first wife is an excellent woman and I'm sure you will be happy in their household."

Jin-Lian stood rooted to the spot. Her legs turned to lead and her face flushed as she bit her lip to hold back her tears. Her throat burned with the effort of forming words and willing them to come out of her mouth.

"Of course, father. Whatever you say. Thank you."

She turned and left the room silently, leaving her father puzzled... why is she not more pleased? I have made her a good match... I'm sure my wife would have agreed with me.

The audience seemed to recognise the inevitability of the father's dilemma: wanting the best for his daughter and getting things terribly wrong. I thought of the many disagreements and misunderstandings with my own daughters when they were teenagers. Ashley seemed to be enjoying this too and I felt a bit more relaxed as well. Now, before I separated the lovers I wanted us all to care about them, to know how much they loved each other. The image of an old Japanese print came to mind, a gently erotic picture of a man and woman resting in the afterglow of sex. I thought also of the sweet pain of illicit love, the heightening of the senses and emotions that comes from knowing that it cannot last.

"Oh Mah Ji-Yan, what are we to do?" They lay on the couch, half-naked and flushed after making love. A warm breeze caressed Jin-Lian's skin, beads of sweat trickled down her stomach. "I cannot disobey my father. He is so good to me. He means well and a daughter cannot disobey her father. I must do what he says."

Mah Ji-Yan stroked the tears from Jin-Lian's cheek and kissed her eyes. "I know you must marry this man but I don't know how I can go on living here, seeing you with him, seeing you have his babies. I could not bear it. How can I live without you?" He held Jin-Lian close, their tears mingling on the pillow until they fell asleep.

As the day of the wedding approached, the lovers became more and more desperate, torn between their love for each other and Jin-Lian's unbreakable duty to obey her father. Finally, Mah Ji-Yan could bear it no longer and decided to leave Rivertown forever. He could not even bring himself to tell Jin-Lian that he was going.

He waited until a cloudy night, when the moon would not betray his actions. Just before midnight, he got up from his pallet bed in his parents' house, put on warm trousers and jacket, picked up the few books he possessed, some food from the kitchen and a few yen that he had saved. He slipped the latch, opened the door silently, turned and silently whispered goodbye to his mother and father, and walked to Jin-Lian's father's house. He stood at the garden gate for a long time, gazing at the closed shutters of Jin-Lian's bedroom. Then, blowing a kiss in her direction, he sighed, turned on his heel and made his way through the town.

I had put myself in Mah Ji-Yan's place and tried to imagine the mixture of contradictory feelings: sadness at leaving his parents and grief at losing Jin-Lian, perhaps a certain relief at having made a decision to go and even a sense of excitement and curiosity about the world beyond Rivertown. I saw him walking slowly, noticing almost as if for the first time the familiar surroundings of the town he has known since his birth believing that he will never see them again.

He walked through the town square, past deserted warehouses and offices, evading the night watchmen, past the fishermen's huts to the riverside where a hundred small boats bobbed and knocked against the wooden piers and jetties. Mah Ji-Yan held his breath as he edged past the nets and pungent piles of fish scales and skins. He selected a narrow punt, and untied its plaited-rope tether. Then all it took was one push of the pole to get it away from the other boats and let the current do its work, moving it steadily downstream, away from Rivertown, towards the sea and a new life.

His heart was broken but still he felt lighter and freer for having made a decision. He was in no hurry and allowed the punt to drift close to the bank. Voles and rats plopped into the water as he passed. Coots and moorhens splashed their wings, herding their broods against the reeds for protection as he passed. Occasionally, a small break in the clouds let the moonlight slip through and glance off the rippling water.

Suddenly I remembered myself as a boy, fishing with my father and brother on the riverbank, stretching out the day until we could no longer see the floats and had to pack up our tackle and walk back to the van groping our way along the darkened footpath. I could almost smell the water, sense its teeming life. I wanted to stay with these images a bit longer but the story would not wait.

After a while, Mah Ji-Yan heard a sound, much louder than the night noises he had become used to. Something, a large animal maybe or someone was following him, making their way downstream along the riverbank. Perhaps he had been discovered - stealing a boat was a serious matter. Maybe a watchman had seen him leave. Maybe one of the fishermen was after him. Maybe an evil spirit wanted to punish him for his crime?

Better to have it out, once and for all, than to worry about it like this. Mah Ji-Yan grasped the pole, plunged it into the water and pushed the punt towards the shore. It grounded itself amongst the reeds and Mah Ji-Yan jumped out onto the bank and waited. In the pitch darkness, the sound grew louder and closer - panting, footsteps running, reeds and bushes pushed apart, and suddenly a large shadow appeared in front of him and a figure crashed against him, knocking him to the ground...

So this is was what Ashley and Sue called a "threshold" moment. The audience want to know what manner of thing has come crashing through the bushes but they are also enjoying not knowing. They want to be held in this space of wonder and anticipation a little longer. So I obliged with a few more seconds of silence. Now it was time.

The clouds parted, the moon shone and into his face peered... Jin-Lian.

"Oh, Mah Ji-Yan. Mah Ji-Yan. I knew you would do something like this. I could not let you leave me. I love you. Take me with you. Please take me with you. Wherever you are going I will come too."

Mah Ji-Yan wrapped her in his arms and covered her in kisses. His heart was fit to burst. "Of course I'll take you. We'll make a new life together. We will always be together."

Then he led Jin-Lian to the punt and held her hand as she stepped over the gunwale. He wrapped his warm coat round her shoulders and pushed the boat out into midstream where the current carried them towards the sea. Three days later they arrived at the bustling seaport at the mouth of the river and Mah Ji-Yan was able to buy them a third class passage on a sea-going junk to another province far away.

They were young and vigorous and intelligent and it was not long before they had established themselves in their new land. Mah Ji-Yan and Jin-Lian married and soon had two children of their own - a boy and a girl - and became quite wealthy as they learned how to trade, how to buy and sell for profit. At first, trinkets they made themselves, then fancy goods made for them by friends and neighbours, then a small army of home workers, until eventually they had established themselves as prosperous merchants. They were healthy, happy and content with their lives.

And that could have been where the story ended except that the audience knew that Mah Ji-Yan and Jin-Lian had run away and that there was unfinished business back in Rivertown.

Besides, beyond a certain age most of us don't really trust "happily ever after". Perhaps, as mature adults, we are readier to look beyond simplistic endings, more willing to engage with the complexities of life knowing that while we live, our stories never really stand still. I found that I was enjoying myself now, in full flow. The story was coming along and I felt confident that I could bring it home safely.

I told the audience how, after several years, Jin-Lian persuaded Mah Ji-Yan that they should all return to make their peace with her father and how, when they arrived in Rivertown, Mah Ji-Yan went on ahead to the familiar house which he found shuttered and silent with white flags - the colour of mourning - hanging from the eaves.

Eventually Jin-Lian's father, stooped with care and old before his time, answered Mah Ji-Yan's knock at the door. "What do you want?"

"We've come back sir. I've brought Jin-Lian to see you - and our children."

"That's impossible," said the old man. He pulled Mah Ji-Yan into the hallway towards a bedroom at the back of the house. "Here," he said. "Look here." He slid open the door. There on the bed lay the gaunt figure of a woman. "The day after you left, she retired to her room. Before long she stopped eating more than a few grains of rice a day. Now she won't even drink water. She is near death."

Now we were in a different kind of story. This twist had presented us with a mystery. I paused, teasing the audience with unspoken questions. Who could this be on the bed? Surely not Jin-Lian? But who else could it be? What on earth would happen now? How could the story find resolution?

Mah Ji-Yan gazed in horror at the still figure on the bed. "Jin-Lian?" he cried out. "Honoured sir, this cannot be true. Jin-Lian is with me, she has come with our children. Wait, I will fetch her now."

He stumbled from the house and ran down the street to meet his wife and children. Wordlessly he pushed Jin-Lian ahead and putting his arms round his son and daughter, watched as his wife approached her father's house. As she reached the garden gate, a pale figure came out of the front door towards her, a second Jin-Lian, wasted with hunger and close to death. The two slowly drew closer until they stood before each other. At the same moment they each reached out toward the other and as their hands touched... they merged and became one.

I brought my own two hands together, enacting this union between the two Jin-Lians and allowed them to remain in an attitude of prayerful silence for a while as the small group of listeners digested the denouement for themselves. Then it was time to bring us all back from the world of the story to this world.

And what has this to do with koans, you may ask? Well, the koan drawn from this story by the Zen masters is "Jin-Lian and her soul are separated. Which is the true one?" What do you think?

Well, I had done it and done it as well as I could. I had especially enjoyed the interplay between the story, images from my trip to China and a more personal sense of connection with some key moments. The group seemed to have liked the story too. Ashley was smiling and I grinned back my delight. Perhaps I was a storyteller after all.

That morning after breakfast Ashley took me to one side. "Sue and I were wondering if you would like to tell your story again - to the whole group this time - to end the course." I was thrilled and terrified at the same time. "Well, yes, if you think it is good enough." "It's a great story," said Ashley, "and you tell it really well. I think it would be a lovely way to finish."

It was a kind of blessing, a moment of recognition and affirmation from a master storyteller to a budding apprentice, an invitation to join the company of storytellers. It was exactly the acknowledgement I craved at exactly the right time. Had it come later or not come at all I would have been disheartened and might have given up. Had it come earlier I would not have been ready and might have shied away from the challenge. But I had glimpsed the technique that is beyond technique, accessing that vast inner resource of the storyteller's own memory, imagination and feeling, and I was ready to begin to think of myself as a storyteller, albeit an apprentice. Of course I accepted Ashley's invitation to tell the story again to the whole course. I haven't stopped telling stories since.

Whatever calling we follow, there comes a time when our desire outstrips our ability. Then, each of us has to find our own way of dealing with the challenge of facing our lack of competence at doing the very thing we most want to do well. Somehow we have to find our own relationship to what we love, our own unique way of bringing ourselves to our work. That, of course, is what the very best teachers help us do. They do not shape us in their image but meet us on the ground of our being so that we learn to express ourselves more fully.

Go find a teacher!

3
Master & Servant

I am told that the most dangerous time for motorists crossing the channel is not the first day when the immediate strangeness of driving on the "other side" of the road keeps the necessity of doing so firmly in the forefront of the mind. Actually, the most common time for a serious collision is the second or third day, when drivers assume that they know what they are doing and relax their concentration before the habit is ingrained. Pride - an unjustified or exaggerated belief in our own importance and abilities - proverbially comes before a fall.

In storytelling too, the most important lessons (as well as sometimes being the most painful) tend to arrive when you are least expecting them, especially when you begin to think you are doing really well. Fortunately, the consequences are not as dire as those that result from driving on the wrong side of the road. It is the ego rather than the body that gets bruised. This can be exactly what a budding storyteller most needs though it may not be welcomed at the time.

For me, the storytelling equivalent of the continental car crash came whilst I was a student on a thirteen-week full-time training course in the art of storytelling at Emerson College. Three of us: Karen (German), Eva (Swedish) and me (English) had got together one evening after supper to practise a jointly told tale, *Vassilisa the Beautiful,* a long and complicated Russian wonder tale.

"No. No! NO! *I* say, 'One day the merchant left home to go off on his travels, leaving Vassilisa alone with her stepmother and stepsisters,' and then *you* come in with, 'It was not long before the stepmother began sending Vassilisa to do errands in the forest hoping that she would run into the witch Baba Yaga.'"

We had been rehearsing for about half an hour, taking turns to tell sections of the story and things were not going well. Karen had already stumbled over her entrance several times and my patience - already stretched thin - had snapped.

How are we ever going to get the story sorted out, I was thinking, if Karen cannot remember her part and Eva keeps arriving late for our practice sessions and sometimes does not turn up at all? Never mind, I knew what I was doing. I knew how to tell my part of the story and I had some good ideas about how Karen and Eva should tell their parts too.

We went on like this for several more rehearsals and the story lurched along. Karen focused on Baba Yaga, Eva on Vassilisa with me desperately trying to hold things together as narrator, merchant and Tsar, increasingly frustrated and puzzled why we kept on falling off the rails. How difficult could this possibly be? We just needed to get a grip.

All too soon it was Friday morning and the time had come for us to tell our story to the whole course. I quickly got into my stride, delivered the opening section quite confidently, sat back while Karen and Eva struggled a bit through their parts and then returned to close with a flourish.

And so Vassilisa married the Tsar and went to live in the palace, taking the kindly old woman with her as a companion. When her father, the merchant, returned from his travels he was overjoyed to discover his daughter's good fortune. As for the little doll, it is said that Vassilisa kept it by her side for the whole of her long life... or at least until it was time for her to pass it on to her own daughter.

But it was flat and I knew it. Our audience of fellow students had been polite but had not really engaged with the performance. I thought that I had done my part quite well but I felt irritated and let down by Karen and Eva. At break time I walked over to the main house for coffee and a fellow student, Frans, drifted alongside me. He was a gifted storyteller and I was interested in his opinion.

"What did you think?" I asked. "A bit flat wasn't it?"

"I could tell you what the matter was," said Frans. "But you won't like it."

"What do you mean?"

"It wasn't generous," said Frans. "Actually, *you* were not generous. You wanted to show us what a good storyteller you are. I think you wanted us to see you as better than Karen and Eva. Technically you were fine, but there was no heart and soul in it. I don't think you really cared about Vassilisa or what happened to her. And if you don't care about the story when you tell it, how can we care as listeners?"

I forced a smile. "Thanks Frans. I'll have to think about that."

I could feel my throat tighten and my face flush as though it had been slapped. Embarrassed, I poured myself a coffee and took it outside into the garden where I sat down alone on the bench seat by the pond. I had tried so hard, made sure that I knew the story, had done my best to craft it. What did he mean, "not generous", "not care"? I thought back over our performance to try and make sense of his comments.

Reluctantly, I had to admit to myself that there was something in what Frans had said. I had felt superior to Karen and Eva, although in hindsight I could see that the story had only come alive with Karen's wild and strange accent for Baba Yaga and Eva's halting vulnerability as Vassilisa. Their telling had been authentic. They had been present in the story and offered it - and themselves - generously to the audience. I had got in the way of the story, made myself more important than the story, got between it and the audience.

I felt ashamed of my earlier frustration with Karen and Eva, ashamed too at my sense of self-importance. I realised that I had arrived at Emerson full of myself: ex-Chief Superintendent of Police, used to taking things in my stride; recently graduated Doctor of Philosophy, literate, articulate, intelligent. Somehow I was letting all this get in the way of being a good storyteller. This was not what I thought I had come to Emerson College to learn. I had expected to develop my storytelling skills, not to question my whole way of being.

Yet I knew that I could not ignore the truth of Frans' words if I really wanted to tell stories.

A few days later, when I felt I had silently chewed on this bone long enough (and after the immediate sting of Frans' words had subsided somewhat), I asked our teacher Ashley what he had to say about getting in the way of the story and what advice he could offer to help me avoid doing it again.

"Serve the story," he said. "The storyteller's sacred task is to serve the story. You have to let the story in, allow yourself to feel and respect its power, let it speak through you, give it away whole-heartedly, be present, stand in its presence and the presence of the listeners. To be a storyteller is to be a servant of the story and not just a master of the craft."

As these words sank in, I realised that *Vassilisa the Beautiful*, Karen, Eva, Frans and Ashley had, between them, taught me a profound lesson. There was really no point telling stories at all unless I was prepared to throw myself into it. Could I risk letting go of most of what I had learned in thirty years as a police officer about staying detached and in control? Could I stand in front of an audience as myself, vulnerable and fallible? Could I feel the power of a story and let it speak through me? I vowed to myself, then and there, that whenever I got the chance to do some storytelling, I would do my best to follow Ashley's dictum: not to worry about how good a storyteller I appeared to be but focus instead on serving the story as well as I could.

Storytellers need a certain amount of ego strength just to stand up in front of an audience and claim the space in which to tell a story but that same ego needs to be tempered: too fragile and the story may not be offered confidently enough for the audience to receive it; too flamboyant and the performance may overshadow the story completely; too needy and the storyteller will be in constant danger of using the audience to bolster their own self-image.

Oral storytelling is relational, it cannot happen in isolation. There are, as Doug Lipman explains so well in *Improving Your Storytelling*[6], three obvious ingredients to a performance: the storyteller, the audience and the story. All three are in relationship with each other but the crucial relationship between the audience and the story is beyond the storyteller's grasp.

As a storyteller, you can create one relationship with the story and another with the audience, but you are powerless to force the audience to create a relationship with the story. You can try to influence that third relationship through the relationships that involve you directly, but you can only prepare, suggest, offer, and then hope.

Lipman also recognises the paradoxical position of the storyteller who must give it everything they've got *and* get out of the way and trust the mystery of a process they can influence but not control.

To succeed at storytelling, then, you need to accept your inability to create this relationship [between audience and story] directly. You need humility. At the same time, you need to make effective use of the tools available to you to foster this relationship. You need persistence, clarity, ingenuity, and caring.

Learning the techniques of storytelling is the easy part, a bit of study and application will do the trick. But if we really want to put on the mantle of the storyteller, we need to commit to a life-long journey of learning, not only about the skills of an ancient craft, but also about how to conduct ourselves as storytellers. And at the heart of it all is our relationship with our selves.

4
A Moment of Grace

You may well ask; if being and becoming a storyteller is so difficult and demanding, why would anyone want to do it? I guess all storytellers would have different answers to that question but one of the reasons I have stayed on this path is that sometimes a story I am telling seems to fly. Something almost magical arises between the teller, the tale and the audience. It brings a quite unpredictable glimpse of the sublime that cannot be forced. Indeed, striving only seems to make it more elusive. But when it happens, it is utterly thrilling and at such times I absolutely know that there is nothing else in the world that I would rather be than a storyteller.

One such moment of grace came several years ago when I travelled to Japan to spend some time with Yoshie, a friend I had met at Emerson College. I flew into Tokyo and then took a coach for the four-hour ride west to Ina, a small town in the foothills of the Japanese Alps where Yoshie lived with her husband. Before my arrival, Yoshie had got together with some of her friends and arranged for me to give several storytelling performances with her in surrounding schools and village halls, culminating in a larger "International Storytelling" event in Ina itself. Sitting on the coach I thought about what lay ahead. Given that I did not speak Japanese and that many of our audience members would have very little English, I wondered how they would react to my stories and whether I could somehow tell them in a way that would make any kind of sense.

During the next week I wrestled with unfamiliar food and chopsticks, learned to sleep soundly on a futon on the hard *tatami*-covered floor, and bowed incessantly and often inappropriately in an effort to be polite. I accidentally ripped the rice-paper panelling of my room, and generally caused much inadvertent hilarity amongst my good-humoured and generous hosts. Above all, I told stories, story after story, to groups of children, to teachers and parents, to complete strangers and to new friends.

The storytelling was every bit as challenging and far more delightful that I had imagined on the journey to Ina. After the final performance, Yoshie and her friends put on a farewell party for me and everyone else involved in organising the trip. As we chatted about the week's events and I thanked my hosts, a woman's voice cut across the hubbub and I heard my name being called (I had been using my middle name as it seemed marginally less un-pronounceable to Japanese tongues).

"Douglas-San, please tell us the story of Jumping Mouse."

The room fell silent and I looked across to see who had spoken. It was Yoko, whose house I had stayed at in nearby Matsumoto for a couple of nights. She looked back at me. "You told us that Jumping Mouse was one of your favourite stories. Please don't go without telling us the story."

She was right. Jumping Mouse was (and is still) a particular favourite of mine and I had given her a porcelain mouse as a keepsake when I had stayed with her. That must have been when I mentioned the story, I thought. I wondered if she really wanted to hear the story or whether her request was some sort of elaborate courtesy that I was unknowingly obliged to decline. As I pondered what to do, she smiled and held my gaze. Then other voices joined hers: Noriko, Yoshie, Akira, Hideko. "Yes, do. Do tell us the story."

I racked my brains. I knew that most people in the room had good enough English to understand it but could I remember the story well enough to tell it there and then without any preparation? Then, a man named Katsumi spoke. "If you tell the story, I will accompany you. I have my flutes here. I know the story well. We could do it together."

A few days before, I had heard Katsumi play the Native American flutes at a concert and I knew that he was a fine musician. What an opportunity, I thought, the chance to tell Jumping Mouse, that great Lakota teaching tale, with authentic music, to people begging to hear it. I looked at my watch. There was just enough time for the story before my bus left for Tokyo. I decided that I would do it. I would just have to trust that the words of the story would come back to me as I needed them.

"Of course," I said. "I would be delighted to tell you the story."

While the small crowd of twenty or so formed itself into an audience, I positioned myself so that I could see beyond them to the windows. Katsumi unwrapped a cloth from a gleaming set of wooden flutes, blew gently to test the notes and made some minute adjustments to alter their pitch.

Katsumi stood slender and tall beside my chair, grey ponytail hanging to his waist. He glanced at me and nodded, ready. I nodded back. Katsumi closed his eyes and began to play: at first the faintest of high warbling breathy notes, then with increasing intensity and volume. After two or three minutes he stopped. The room was filled with pregnant silence. I looked at the audience, gathering them in with my eyes, drew a deep breath, exhaled and began.

Once (some say long ago and some say not) there was a little mouse. He lived in a briar patch that had grown up around the stump of a tumbled-down cottonwood tree at the edge of the great prairie on the plains of North America. Though he was busy, once in a while he heard or thought he heard an odd sound. If he stopped for a moment, lifted his head and pricked his ears, there seemed to be a roaring sound coming from far away. Nothing in the briar patch made such a noise and he wondered what it could be. He puzzled over it for a long time. Perhaps one of his fellow mice knew what caused the sound?

We were off and I realised that I need not have worried about remembering the story. It was all there and the music was bringing a new intensity and power to the words and images. I paused for a moment to check that the audience was with us. They seemed intent and as enraptured by the music as I had been. I picked up from where I had left off and on we went together. From time to time, Katsumi improvised in response to the story and, in turn, my telling lifted the story in response to the music. It felt as though we were playing a duet, point and counterpoint, each inspiring the other and each inspired by the story. The world of the story opened up in my imagination and I stepped inside. I could see the landscape, hear the rushing waters of the river, smell the scent of the grass, feel the warmth of the sun, and taste the very substance of the words.

"You have come a long way to find this place, little brother. Would you like to have some Medicine Power?" asked Frog.

"Medicine Power? Me?" Little Mouse was astonished. "Yes please. I should like that very much."

"Then crouch down as low as you can then jump as high as you can and you will have your Medicine Power," said Frog.

Little Mouse did as he was instructed. He crouched as low as he could and jumped with all his might, as high as he could. As he hung for a moment suspended in mid-air at the point between rising and falling, his eyes were drawn to the East and there he saw, very faint and far off, half-hidden among clouds and covered in snow, the Sacred Mountains. He could hardly believe his eyes, yet there they were.

As I said these words, I looked beyond the audience, through the window and out towards the Japanese Alps, their tops still covered with late winter snow, glorious in the afternoon sunlight. "Look," I said. "There they are, the Sacred Mountains." I stood up and pointed out of the window. The audience turned their heads and we gazed together for a long moment at the mountains amongst which they lived out their daily lives. There was a collective intake of breath as if, I thought, they were seeing the mountains for the first time. The hairs on the back of my neck stood up, my skin tingled and suddenly I knew that they too had entered the world of the story. I could sense that now we were all looking through the eyes of Jumping Mouse and that we would follow him faithfully through every danger and every sacrifice, across the wide prairie, to the very end of his quest.

Jumping Mouse and the other creatures of the story - raccoon, frog, buffalo, wolf, eagle - seemed to come alive in the room. I could feel the story flow through me and I heard my own voice as if it were someone else speaking. I did not have to try to remember who did what or what happened next. I was just witnessing the story unfolding and sharing it. After journeying together for what could have been minutes, hours or days, we arrived at the fateful moment.

Jumping Mouse heard the shrill, piercing cries of a hunting eagle above him. The sound stopped suddenly and he knew that he had been spotted. He sensed the approaching shadow and felt the wind of the eagle's wings on his back. A thrill of fear and joy passed through his body and he braced himself for the shock.

The eagle hit!

Jumping Mouse went to sleep.

A long time passed and then he woke up. He was astonished to be alive. What is more, he could see. Everything was blurry but the light and the colours were dazzling.

"I can see. I can see," he said, over and over again.

A faint green and white shape came towards him. He squinted hard but it stayed fuzzy.

"Hello, brother," said a voice that was strangely familiar. "Would you like to have some Medicine Power?"

"Yes please. I should like that very much."

"Then crouch down as low as you can," the voice said. "And jump as high as you can and you will have your Medicine Power."

Jumping Mouse crouched as low as he could and jumped with all his might, as high as he could. He hung for a moment suspended in mid-air at the point between rising and falling. This time the wind caught him and carried him higher.

"Don't be afraid," said the voice. "Hang on to the wind and trust!"

Jumping Mouse trusted. He hung on to the wind and it carried him higher and higher. As he rose up, he could see more and more

clearly. He looked down and saw his old friend far below sitting on
a lily pad on the beautiful Medicine Lake.

"Is that you, Frog?" he called.

"Hello, Jumping Mouse," cried Frog. "Look… look at yourself."

Jumping Mouse looked. Where his hind legs had been were
sharp talons, where his forelegs had been were wing feathers and
where his nose and whiskers had been was a great curved beak.

"You have a new name," called Frog. "You are Eagle now."

Eagle spread his wings wide and he flew… and he flew… and
he flew.

The story ended. Katsumi played again, the notes hovering, soaring, carrying us through the air, and supporting us in imagined flight just as the wind had taken Jumping Mouse higher and higher. As the last notes died away the room fell silent. I looked around at the audience and I could see that many of them had tears in their eyes. Some of them reached out to hold each other's shoulders. Katsumi put down his flutes, and threw his arms round me. We knew that we had all been touched by grace.

There was just time to make our farewells before I caught the coach back to Tokyo for my flight home. As the bus ate up the miles, I sipped a can of hot sweet coffee and stared out of the window at Mount Fuji projecting itself through low clouds, to hang like some fairytale castle unsupported in the sky. I thought of Jumping Mouse and bathed in the wonder and mystery of what had happened in that unremarkable room in Ina just a few hours before. Then I remembered Ashley's words at Emerson College years before: "The storyteller's sacred task is to serve the story."

And in serving the story - without any expectation - my reward was to be part of something remarkable: a deep sense of communion in which the landscape, the audience and the performers had become one with the story. We found the world of the story in us and we found ourselves in the world of the story. For a brief time, our fates and the fate of *Jumping Mouse* became entwined and we could draw strength and inspiration from our shared quest to find the Sacred Mountains. His transformation into Eagle offered each one of us the challenge and the possibility of finding our own transformation into the highest and best that we could become.

Times like this come unbidden when we have done our work, developed our skills, learned our stories, invested them with our imagination, and shared them with a generous heart. They are, I believe, the true and ample reward of those who commit themselves to being and becoming storytellers.

Jumping Mouse

Once (some say long ago and some say not) there was a little mouse. He lived in a briar patch that had grown up around the stump of a tumbled-down cottonwood tree at the edge of the great prairie on the plains of North America. Little Mouse was busy, busy as all mice are, scurrying around with his nose to the ground, whiskers twitching, looking for seeds and fallen fruit to eat and dry grass for bedding, passing the time of day with his brothers and sisters, his cousins, his aunts and uncles, and all the other mice who shared the briar patch.

Though he was busy, once in a while he heard or thought he heard an odd sound. If he stopped for a moment, lifted his head and pricked his ears, there seemed to be a roaring sound coming from far away. Nothing in the briar patch made such a noise and he wondered what it could be. He puzzled over it for a long time. Perhaps one of his fellow mice knew what caused the sound?

One day he stopped one of his cousins and asked, "Do you hear a roaring sound in your ears?" But his cousin hurried on without lifting his nose from the ground. "Hear nothing. Busy now. Hear nothing." He asked one of his aunts the same question. She stopped for a moment and looked at him. "What sound? There is no sound. Are you soft in the head?" Then his aunt slipped away into her nest under a fallen branch and was gone.

Little Mouse twitched his whiskers and shrugged. Perhaps he was soft in the head, he thought. He would get back to his busyness and forget the whole thing. But no matter how hard he tried to forget, the sound would not go away. Every time he stopped and listened he could hear the same roar. It was faint, very faint, but it was definitely there.

So he left the other busy mice and went to the very edge of the briar patch where he could be alone. There was the sound again, as clear as day. He shut his eyes and listened hard. Suddenly, right behind him, a voice boomed "Hello."

Little Mouse almost jumped out of his skin. He arched his back, *ready to run, when the voice spoke again. "Hello, little brother. It's me, Raccoon." Little Mouse looked and sure enough, there was Raccoon with his dark eye patches and striped tail, towering over him. He looked friendly enough. "What are you doing here all by yourself, little brother?"*

"I hear a roaring sound in my ears and I'm er... I'm investigating it," said Little Mouse blushing with a mixture of embarrassment and sudden pride. "That's what I'm doing, investigating."

Raccoon sat down on his haunches beside him. "A roaring sound in your ears, eh? What you hear, little brother, is the river."

"Ri-ver," Little Mouse said. "What's a ri-ver?"

"Well," said Raccoon. "It's a... it's a kind of... it's more like... It's very hard to describe. But if you walk with me I can show you."

Little Mouse wasn't sure what to do. He had never been away from the briar patch. The thought of leaving the only world he knew was terrifying but he was determined to find out once and for all about the roaring sound. I know it is real, he thought. No-one believed me but I will see this thing for myself and then I will prove to them all that I am not soft in the head. Besides, this thing might help me with all my busyness. "Thank you, Brother Raccoon, I would like to see the river. I will walk with you."

Raccoon turned and led the way down an unfamiliar path, away from the briar patch towards the roaring sound. The path was full of strange scents and several times Little Mouse was sure he glimpsed eyes looking at him sideways through the brush. His heart pounded in his chest and he felt like turning back. He kept close to Raccoon who talked cheerfully of this and that and seemed quite unafraid.

The roaring sound grew louder and louder so that it became quite difficult to hear Raccoon speaking. Eventually, the path opened out and there before them was the river. It was huge, bigger than anything Little Mouse had ever seen. It was so wide that he could not see across it to the other side. A great torrent of golden-green water rushed past them, carrying clods of earth and broken branches on its back. And the noise: it roared, it cried, it sang, it thundered on its way. Raccoon bent down and Little Mouse yelled in his ear, "It's wonderful, it's so... powerful."

"It is a great thing," Raccoon yelled back. "Come with me, there

is someone here I want you to meet." He led the way to a quieter, shallower part of the river where they could hear each other much better. "Let me introduce you," he said and jerked his head in the direction of a lily pad bobbing on the surface of the water some distance from the bank. Sitting on one of the leaves was a bright green frog with a white belly.

"Hello, little brother," said Frog. "Welcome to the river."

"I have to go now," said Raccoon to his companion. "But don't worry. Frog will look after you." And Raccoon wandered off along the river bank looking for food that he could wash and eat.

Little Mouse made his way to the water's edge and peered down. He saw his own frightened reflection peering back. He quickly looked up again and called out. "Hello, Frog. Aren't you afraid to be so far out into the Great River?"

Frog laughed. "No, I'm not afraid. The Maker gave me the gift of being able to live both above and within the river. You won't find me when winter comes and turns everything to ice but for the rest of the year, when the world is green, I am here. I am the keeper of the water."

"Amazing," said Little Mouse. "You must be a great being and to think that I never knew about you or even about the Great River."

"You have come a long way to find this place, little brother. Would you like to have some Medicine Power?" asked Frog.

"Medicine Power? Me?" Little Mouse was astonished. "Yes please. I should like that very much."

"Then crouch down as low as you can then jump as high as you can and you will have your Medicine Power," said Frog.

Little Mouse did as he was instructed. He crouched as low as he could and jumped with all his might, as high as he could. He seemed to move in slow motion and his senses came alive as though he could smell, hear and see all the scents, sounds and sights of the world. As he hung for a moment suspended in mid-air at the point between rising and falling, his eyes were drawn to the East and there he saw, very faint and far off, half-hidden among clouds and covered in snow, the Sacred Mountains. He could hardly believe his eyes, yet there they were.

Then gravity took hold and he fell back down, landing not on the earth but in the river. He coughed and spluttered and scrabbled his way to the bank, terrified that he would drown. "You tricked me," he screamed at Frog.

"Wait," said Frog. "You are not harmed. Don't let your fear and anger get the better of you. Tell me, what did you see?"

"I did see something," said the mouse, still wet and shaking. "I saw the Sacred Mountains. They were far away to the East where the sun rises. They were wonderful." His voice trailed off as he thought of them.

"Indeed," said Frog. "Now you have your Medicine Power you shall have a new name. It is Jumping Mouse."

"Thank you. Thank you," said Jumping Mouse, squirming with excitement. It was almost more than he could bear. "I must go back and tell my people of these things that I have seen: the Great River and the Sacred Mountains."

"If you are sure that is what you want to do," said Frog. "Just turn around and go back the way you came. Keep the sound of the river behind you and you won't get lost. By all means tell your people but don't be surprised if they don't believe you."

So Jumping Mouse returned to his own familiar world to tell his fellow mice about what had happened to him and the wonders he had seen. But Frog had been right, no-one wanted to hear. Worse still, he frightened them. "Your fur is wet," said one. "It's not been raining and your fur is wet. Some animal has tried to eat you and they spat you out. You must be poisonous. Keep away from us."

Jumping Mouse stayed with his people for a while, hoping that they would listen or at least accept him back as one of them. He even told himself that in time his vision of the Sacred Mountains would fade. But it did not; the memory of what he had seen burned more and more strongly in his heart and mind. He longed to see them again and one day he knew what he must do. He took himself to the edge of the briar patch and looked out at the prairie – a great green ocean of grass sweeping away to the horizon. He looked up into the sky for eagles. He saw many black dots wheeling high overhead, each one an eagle and he knew that outside the shelter of the briar patch he would be completely exposed, easy prey for any bird that spotted him.

Yet, no matter the danger, he was determined to find the Sacred Mountains. His little heart pounded with fear and excitement but he gathered all his courage and launched himself out amongst the prairie grass running as far and as fast as he could go, towards the rising sun.

He kept going until he could go no further and just when he was about to collapse from exhaustion he stumbled into a clump of sage bushes. Cover at last! Jumping Mouse stopped running and tried to catch his breath. After a little while he looked around. There were seeds to eat and grass and dry sage leaves on the ground for nesting material: a haven for mice. As he wandered about the place he saw another mouse, a very old mouse.

"Hello," said Old Mouse. "Welcome to my home."

"Thank you," said Jumping Mouse. "This is a wonderful place. You must be a truly great mouse to have found your way here and made it your home."

"It is the perfect spot," said Old Mouse. "The eagles cannot see us but we can look out at all the creatures of the prairie and know their names: the buffalo, antelope, rabbit and coyote. You can see them all from here."

"Can you also see the Sacred Mountains?" asked Jumping Mouse. "I am on my way there. I went to the Great River and I saw them far away."

"Ah, yes. The Great River. I went there myself, many years ago. But the Sacred Mountains are just a dream, they don't really exist, you know. Why don't you stay here with me? There is everything you could possibly want, right here."

"How can he say such a thing?" thought Jumping Mouse. The Medicine Power of the Sacred Mountains was not something to be denied. "Thank you for your kind offer but I must continue my journey as soon as I have rested."

"You are a fool to leave," said Old Mouse. "The prairie is a dangerous place. Think of all those eagles, one of them is bound to catch you. Is that how you want to end your days, as breakfast for an eagle? Well, well. Go if you must."

Once again, Jumping Mouse gathered his courage and launched himself out into the ocean of grass, running as fast as his legs would carry him, ducking and diving behind stones and scrubby plants for cover whenever he could. The shadows of the eagles high in the sky followed him wherever he went. He imagined them looking down at him as he ran on and on, further than he thought he could possibly go. At last, as his legs gave way beneath him, he found himself safe once more, in a stand of chokecherries.

It was spacious and cool amongst the trees. There was water to drink, cherries and seeds to eat, grasses to gather and holes for nests, enough to keep a mouse busy for several lifetimes. As Jumping Mouse explored his new domain he suddenly became aware of the sound of heavy breathing. It was slow and laboured and seemed to be coming from a huge mound of hair, hooves and horns in a nearby clearing. He inched his way forward. It was a buffalo, lying on the ground, so large that a whole family of mice might have made their home in one of its horns. Such a magnificent being, thought Jumping Mouse and crept even closer.

"Hello, little brother," said Buffalo, slowly raising his great head. "Thank you for coming to see me."

"Hello, great being," said Jumping Mouse. "Why are you lying on the ground? What is wrong with you?"

"I am sick," said Buffalo. "Only one thing can cure me: the eye of a mouse. But I don't think there is such a thing as a mouse, I've certainly never seen one myself. So I will stay here until I die."

One of my eyes! Jumping Mouse gulped. One of my tiny eyes!

He scurried out of the clearing and hid behind the trunk of a tree. What was he to do? Buffalo's breathing seemed to get harder and slower: sharp, shuddering in-breaths followed by long, sighing out-breaths. If I do not give him one of my eyes he will die, thought Jumping Mouse. He is too great a being for me to let die. Slowly, he made his way back into the clearing and spoke to Buffalo in a shaky voice.

"There is such a creature as a mouse. I am a mouse and you, my brother, are a great being. I cannot let you die. I have two eyes, please take one of them."

No sooner were the words out of his mouth than his left eye flew out of his head and Buffalo was cured. He got to his feet and lowered his head to speak to the little mouse. "Thank you, little brother. Now I am whole again, I know who you are. You are Jumping Mouse, you went to see the Great River and now you are on a quest to find the Sacred Mountains. You have given me life and I will be your brother forever. If you wish, I will take you across the prairie to where the mountains begin. Follow my footsteps, walk beneath my belly and the eagles will not see you. You will be quite safe with me until we get there but I cannot take you further than the foothills because the Maker decided that I should live on the plains. I might fall on you if I try to go up into the mountains. Will you walk with me?"

"I will walk with you," said Jumping Mouse, peering up with his one good eye. "Thank you." So they set off together. The little mouse ran along in Buffalo's shadow, dodging his sharp hooves. He was relieved that the eagles could not see him but feared at every earth-shaking footfall that he would be crushed. Each night they rested, Jumping Mouse curled safely in Buffalo's shaggy coat and each morning they set off again towards the rising sun. Eventually, after many days and nights, Buffalo stopped. "This is where I must leave you, little brother. You can go on but I must stay on the prairie."

"Thank you, great one," said Jumping Mouse. "I would not have got this far without you even though I was frightened that your hooves might have crushed me."

"You need not have feared," said Buffalo. "I always know where my hooves will fall, you were in no danger. I wish you well on your journey. You can find me here if ever you have need of me. I will always be your friend. Farewell."

Buffalo turned and walked off and Jumping Mouse looked East once more. Though his vision was poor he could see that he had arrived at the edge of a great forest of pine trees, sloping up and away into the distance. He had arrived at the foothills of the Sacred Mountains. Surely nothing could stop him now. He made his way among the ancient pines, always moving up the slope. The mighty tree trunks stretched up out of sight as if they had grown there to keep the sky from falling. Everywhere he looked, he found water to drink, food to eat, plenty of places to build nests and soft pine needles to sleep on. It was a veritable paradise and he might have stayed there had not the memory of his vision of the snow-covered mountains burned inside him like hot coals.

Jumping Mouse made slow but steady progress up the foothills until, one day, in a clearing in the forest he came upon the grey figure of a timber wolf. The wolf was sitting perfectly still, panting *gently. Its head hung low, ears drooping, tongue lolling out. Its eyes were dim with a far-away look in them.*

"Hello, brother wolf," said Jumping Mouse.

At the sound of his voice, the wolf's ears pricked up and he raised his head, eyes shining. "Wolf! Wolf! Yes, that is what I am, I am a wolf!" But quickly, the wolf's mind dimmed and he sat quite still as before, seemingly with no memory of who or what he was. Each time Jumping Mouse spoke, the wolf briefly came to life but immediately slumped back into a torpor.

"Such a great being," *thought Jumping Mouse.* "But he has forgotten himself."

The little mouse went to the edge of the clearing. He listened to the beating of his heart for a long time, deep in thought. Suddenly he made up his mind and scurried back to where the wolf sat, stock still.

"Brother Wolf," *said Jumping Mouse.*

"Wolf! Wolf!" *said the wolf.*

"Listen to me Brother Wolf. I know what will heal you: my eye. You are a great being and I want to give it to you. Please take it." *No sooner had the words left his mouth than Jumping Mouse's remaining eye flew out of his head and Wolf was made whole. Tears fell down Wolf's cheeks but his little brother could not see them, for now he was blind.*

"Thank you," *said Wolf.* "The Maker gave you a great spirit. I am the guide to the Sacred Mountains and now I have my memory back I will take you there. At the very heart of the mountains is the Medicine Lake. Everything in the world is reflected in its surface: the people and their lodges and all the creatures of the prairies and skies. If you come with me I will take you there and describe to you all that can be seen. Will you walk with me?"

"I will walk with you," *said Jumping Mouse.* "Though I don't know how as I can no longer see."

Wolf knelt down close to the little mouse and laid his great head on the ground. Jumping Mouse twitched his whiskers and sniffed the air then he shuffled forward and climbed into Wolf's thick grey neck-fur. "Hold tight," *said Wolf and stood up. Then he turned uphill and with Jumping Mouse holding on for dear life, he loped through the forest, up above the tree-line and into the heart* of the Sacred Mountains. When they reached the Medicine Lake, he lay down his head once more and Jumping Mouse crawled out and crouched on the earth, screwing up his blind eye-sockets against the unseen glare of the sun.

As he had promised, Wolf described the wonders that were reflected in the surface of the lake. Jumping Mouse imagined them all, as if they had passed through his mind. Then Wolf said "I will stay here with you always and keep you safe."

"You cannot do that," said Jumping Mouse. "You are the guide to the Sacred Mountains. How will others find their way here if you do not return to the foothills? It is true that I am frightened to be alone here but you must go."

"You are right, wise one," said Wolf. "I will leave you here by the water's edge so that you may drink from the Medicine Lake. I am proud to call you Brother and I will always be your friend. Farewell."

Wolf left and Jumping Mouse crouched by the lakeside, trembling in fear. He could not run for he was blind and he knew that an eagle would surely find him here, out in the open, high up in the mountains. He smelt the cool water of the lake and eased forward to slake his thirst. As he drank, his heartbeat slowed and his fear subsided. He thought back over his long journey and waited calmly for his fate.

He heard the shrill, piercing cries of a hunting eagle above him. The sound stopped suddenly and he knew that he had been spotted. He sensed the approaching shadow and felt the wind of the eagle's wings on his back. A thrill of fear and joy passed through his body and he braced himself for the shock.

The eagle hit!

Jumping Mouse went to sleep.

A long time passed and then he woke up. He was astonished to be alive. What is more, he could see. Everything was blurry but the light and the colours were dazzling.

"I can see. I can see," he said, over and over again.

A faint green and white shape came towards him. He squinted hard but it stayed fuzzy.

"Hello, brother," said a voice that was strangely familiar. "Would you like to have some Medicine Power?"

"Yes please. I should like that very much."

"Then crouch down as low as you can," the voice said. "And jump as high as you can and you will have your Medicine Power."

Jumping Mouse crouched as low as he could and jumped with all his might, as high as he could. He hung for a moment suspended in mid-air at the point between rising and falling. This time the wind caught him and carried him higher.

"Don't be afraid," said the voice. "Hang on to the wind and trust!"

Jumping Mouse trusted. He hung on to the wind and it carried him higher and higher. As he rose up, he could see more and more clearly. He looked down and saw his old friend far below sitting on a lily pad on the beautiful Medicine Lake.

"Is that you, Frog?" he called.

"Hello, Jumping Mouse," cried Frog. "Look… look at yourself."

Jumping Mouse looked. Where his hind legs had been were sharp talons, where his forelegs had been were wing feathers and where his nose and whiskers had been was a great curved beak.

"You have a new name," called Frog. "You are Eagle now."

Eagle spread his wings wide and he flew… and he flew… and he flew.

About the story

This great Lakota teaching story has been shared with non-Native American cultures by Hyemeyohsts Storm, in his classic book of the Plains Indian People, *Seven Arrows* (published by Ballantine Books, New York). The text, as it appears here, was developed over many years telling the story, and is quite faithful to Storm's original version.

Healing Fictions

*The way we imagine our lives is the way we are going to
go on living our lives. For the manner in which we tell
ourselves about what is going on is the genre through which
events become experiences.*

James Hillman

5
In Bed with the Bear

As storytellers, we learn to open ourselves to the possibility that the stories we tell - the myths, legends, wonder tales, fairy stories, and folktales - are somehow related to our stories, that they have something to say about the ways in which we are living our own lives. To tell a story well, we must empathise with the characters and their fates, we have to imagine what it would be like to be them and what it would be like if we shared their journeys. With a gesture that brings to mind the double loop sign for infinity (∞) we have to find ourselves in the story and find the story in ourselves at the same time. It is only a small step from there to realise that the stories we tell ourselves (and the world) about who we are, both reflect who we are now and shape who we are becoming.

The chapters in this section of the book move beyond storytelling-as-performance to explore the healing potential of storytelling. They look, in a very practical way, at how we can begin to heal some of the wounds and inner divisions we all carry, through stories and storytelling. I am not using the word healing in a pathological sense to signify curing sickness or disease. Rather, I am talking about renewal, about metaphorically finding gold in the ashes of our lives. As Robert Bly says in his poem *A Home in Dark Grass*:[7]

> *We did not come to remain whole*
> *We came to lose our leaves like trees.*
> *The trees that are broken*
> *And start again, drawing up from the great roots.*

As a storyteller, I am especially interested in the relationship between our everyday "real life" stories (which we might call the mundane) and traditional archetypal stories (which we might call the mythic). I am interested in what happens when we tell our mundane stories in mythic form and what we can learn from the wisdom of these ancient tales that can help us in our day-to-day lives. But before we try and help others find healing, it behoves us to attend to our own lives and stories. Storyteller, heal thyself.

When, soon after I began telling stories, I saw an advertisement for a week-long residential storytelling course called *In Bed with the Bear*, I could not resist. It was held at Hawkwood College in Stroud. Ashley Ramsden and Sue Hollingsworth, tutors from the School of Storytelling, led the week and each day they told successive episodes of an old Norwegian wonder tale, *The White Bear King Valemon*. Daily, we followed the fortunes of the princess who married, lost and eventually found again her beloved bear king and, through the power of her love, released him from the Hag Queen's enchantment.

The course offered everything a beginning storyteller could want: working with a fascinating traditional story, voice coaching, exercises in spontaneous storytelling and the chance to tell stories ourselves. Wonderful, but in spite of all these riches, I was despondent and struggling. When it started on Saturday afternoon, all of us participants had been invited to prepare a story during the week to tell on the following Thursday evening at an informal ceilidh. I scoured book after book but nothing grabbed my attention. Uppermost in my mind was just how disturbed I felt being back at Hawkwood. Eighteen months before, I had met someone at an event there. This had resulted in me leaving my marriage. I was separated from my wife and children and divorce was imminent. That was the dominant issue in my life at that time and the prospect of standing up and telling some sort of traditional tale felt trite and cowardly. If I was going to tell a story then, I decided, it would have to be about that - or nothing.

Nothing seemed like an attractive option. I only knew that the story of my life had fallen apart and that I needed to find a new one. The stories that I been used to telling myself about being a dutiful husband and loving father had become hollow and false. Most of the friends and colleagues I had tried to talk to about this were only too ready to project stereotyped stories onto me: a "mid-life cliché story" said dismissive acquaintances; a "great escape story" said those who saw themselves trapped in loveless relationships; a story of "betrayal and desertion" said my wife and children. All these stories (especially the latter) no doubt had some truth in them but they were not my story. I was sick of bobbing around amongst the flotsam and jetsam of my shattered life stories. As I sat there leafing through storybooks it dawned on me that I was the only one who could do anything about it.

Late on Wednesday evening when everyone else had gone up to bed, I took a mug of tea and sat downstairs in the empty group room. The last light of the summer sky faded into night outside as I pondered my story. What on earth was I going to say? An hour passed. I couldn't think of anything that resembled a story. I forced myself to speak out loud to get out of my head, to escape from the tyranny of stale thoughts. For want of anything better, I seized on the opening words of *The White Bear King Valemon*, "Once upon a time, there was a king who had three daughters."

Well that's no use. I'm not a king and besides I have two sons and two daughters. "Once upon a time, there was a king who had two sons and two daughters."

No, that's not it. I'm not a king. I've never been a bloody king. That's what really matters - I've never been a king. During all those years of marriage I have never felt like I was a king, not the king of my own realm. I've been a fraud, a pretender to the throne, someone who once tried to live as if he was a king. Maybe that is my story: the story of a man who stopped pretending he was a king and started to learn who he really was and what he really loved.

"There was once a man who lived as a king." The sound of my voice bounces back from the walls. The words rang true and I decided that would be my starting point. I would tell my story in the form of a fairy tale.

I said the words over and over again. New phrases, even whole sentences came into my mouth and added to the story. Sometimes they didn't sound right and I dropped them, they were too pretentious, too self-pitying, too disparaging, or too whimsical. Several times I got sick of the whole thing and started over again from the very beginning. It became a kind of obsession. Eventually I stumbled across a closing image for the life I was making that satisfied me: planting seeds that shoot and bud and blossom. It had begun to get light outside. I looked at my watch. Christ! It was 4.30 in the morning. I had done enough and, exhausted, I climbed the stairs for a few hours sleep before breakfast.

After lunch I went for a solitary walk in the grounds and told the story to myself again to hone the words and lodge them securely in my memory. My body tingled as I reflected on how important this was to me: this was my life that I was telling. That evening we had the ceilidh. I was on second to last and when my turn came I walked to the chair in the centre of the makeshift stage. My heart was beating fast, I was sweating and my hands were trembling. I sat down and looked at the audience - the twenty or so course members and tutors gathered round the storyteller's chair. I cleared my throat, took a shallow breath and began:

There was once a man who lived as a king. The land in which he was born was rich and fertile. But when he was four years old his father died, and the land died with him. Nothing grew. It became bleak and barren.

When he became a young man he left that place and went to a great university where he studied the history of the ancient kingdoms. While he was there, as sometimes happens to young men, he met a princess. Her father had also died so there was no one to set him ordeals or tests for her hand. However, they were young and they liked each other and they decided to marry.

After the wedding, he moved into her realm. There he found a crown to wear, but it did not fit him very well. Indeed, neither of their crowns fitted very well. They did not know how to rule at all, although they did their best. Since they were young and healthy it was not too long before they had children. In fact they had four wonderful children, two girls and two boys.

You might think that would be enough for anyone's happiness. But they were not happy. For, although they loved their children dearly, they were not secure in each other's love. The years passed. The princess became a queen and turned her love and attention towards the children. The man, not knowing what to do, fell into a deep despair.

Then, one night, he had a dream. He saw the land of his birth and longed to return although he had long since forgotten how to get there. The dream stayed with him and he decided to search for the way. He began to travel out from the queen's court for one or two days, sometimes a week, at a time, visiting new places, meeting new people, even sampling new customs. He regained some of the love of learning that he had as a young man. One thing in particular brought him some respite from his sadness - he learned to dance! There was no dancing in the queen's court but he danced in secret whenever he could. And he went on searching.

One day, as the man approached his fiftieth year, he found himself in a place that he had never been to before. A large stone house perched high on a hill, overlooking a broad valley. There was a great company of people there: scholars, musicians, travellers, searchers like himself. He had a wonderful time. He enjoyed himself so much that he invited them all to join him for a dance that evening.

At dusk they gathered in the ballroom and as the music played they began to dance, some in couples, some alone. Suddenly from the shadows, into the centre of the room, came a beautiful girl. She had a mane of chestnut hair that fell to her waist and swayed as she moved. Her dark eyes flashed with fire and her face shone with good humour. She was wild and free. She called no man her master and she came and went as she pleased. Their eyes met and she approached him boldly. They danced together. They danced and danced and danced out of the evening and into the night.

It was late the next day when the man awoke. He was lying on a grassy bank, under a sycamore tree, with the sun streaming *through its branches onto his face. He was so mesmerised by this sight that he thought that it had all been a dream and he went to turn over. Something held him back and there looking back at him, lying in the crook of his arm, was that same girl.*

Now, she was a spinner of tales and a weaver of spells and she wove a purple bubble around them both to keep out the world. They lay in that place all day, talking, laughing and holding each other close. To him she seemed like a butterfly, free on the wind whilst he was earthbound, stuck in the cocoon. She told him that anything is possible if you want it enough. Eventually the bubble burst, as all bubbles do and the man returned to the queen's court thinking that he should never see the girl again.

As the weeks passed he thought about her more and more and he realised that if he was ever to find his way back to the land of his birth he must first take off his borrowed crown and set it aside. He decided to tell the queen that he was leaving. She was angry and wept bitter tears. He told the children too and they begged him to stay. But he knew that he must go.

And go he did. He walked out of the queen's court with just a few books, a little money and the clothes on his back and he went on walking until he found himself beside a lake. There he built himself a modest home and there he found work, writing and teaching and there he planted many seeds. As the seasons came and went, the seeds sent forth shoots. The shoots swelled into buds, and the buds blossomed.

He began, at last, to live his own life. His days were joyful and full of small adventures. His nights were peaceful and solitary - except when the wild girl came to visit and then the days were full of playful laughter and the nights rang with sweet music.

As the story unfolded, it must have been clear to everyone in the audience that it was my story that I was telling. I saw acceptance in their warm smiles and saw myself, my new self, mirrored in their moist eyes. When I finished, Sue and Ashley hugged me and I felt as though I had taken the first steps to reclaim my identity. The next day I wrote the story down pretty much as it appears here and in the following weeks and months I told it several more times. For a long time

I continued to feel its support as I strove to rebuild my life in very different circumstances.

Of course, my story was not the truth, certainly not the exclusive truth. Other characters - my ex-wife, our children, even the "wild girl" - would, I am sure, have told different stories. I also recognised as time went on that while it had served me well in the wake of separation and divorce it too needed to change. By now ten years have passed, and the "wild girl" and I are long parted. I have experienced other significant changes in my life and I have had to keep on finding other stories, ones that reflect where I am now and where I might be going in my sixties.

Looking back, I realise that following the breakdown of my marriage I was experiencing what (I later discovered) Arthur Frank calls narrative wreckage: times when our sense of self gets shattered, when our lives "hit the rocks" and the familiar stories we tell about ourselves don't make sense anymore. I think that many people experience this condition some time in their lives, perhaps in the wake of traumatic events such as divorce, bereavement, redundancy or illness. The way out of narrative wreckage, says Frank in *The Wounded Storyteller*:

> *...is telling stories, specifically... self-stories. The self-story is not told for the sake of description, though description may be its ostensible content. The self is being formed in what is told.*[8]

This was one of the most difficult times of my life, but fortunately I came to understand that in the dissolution of my old identity was an opportunity to live into a different story. I also sensed that the quality and nature of the new story that I told would be fateful. It would have been quite possible (perhaps even quite tempting) to be self-aggrandising or self-deluding. In hindsight, I can see that the prospect of telling the story to an audience helped to keep me on the straight and narrow. In the event, I discovered that having listeners was crucially important. In telling my story to them I was actually telling it to myself, and the caring quality of their attention greatly amplified the healing power of the story. As Frank says:

> *The moral genius of storytelling is that each, teller and listener, enters the space of the story for the other. Telling stories in post-modern times, and perhaps in all times, attempts to change one's own life by affecting the lives of others. Thus all stories have an element of testimony.*[9]

With the encouragement and support of my fellow storytellers at Hawkwood, I was able to create the kind of story that James Hillman calls a healing fiction, one that enabled me to re-imagine my life in a new and positive way. By weaving particular events from my life into story form, I gave them new meaning and created new imaginative possibilities for myself.

6
Stories all the Way Down

When I told my personal story of building a new life after separation and divorce as the story of *The Man Who Lived as a King*, I had accidentally stumbled upon the idea that our identity is not fixed and that throughout our lives we continually create (and recreate) our sense of who we are through the stories we tell about ourselves. This, of course, is the domain of psychotherapy but I began to wonder how as storytellers (not as therapists) we might offer people opportunities to re-story aspects of their lives in respectful and helpful ways.

It occurred to me that a straightforward way to begin would be to invite people to explore their early childhood connection with story and storytelling. I set up a workshop at the University of Bath where at the time I was studying for my PhD. Twenty of us gathered in a plain, whitewashed, seminar room with empty bookshelves on the walls. All of us had some connection with academic life - professors, lecturers, and doctoral students - so we could not have claimed to be a random sample[10]. We agreed to record the event for research purposes and I undertook to maintain the anonymity of the participants. I kicked things off with the following instruction:

Take a deep breath. Think back to your early childhood, to when you first became aware that there were stories. See if you can imaginatively connect with that time. Were stories told when you were a child? Or was there an absence of stories? What was your favourite story in your childhood? How did it come to you? Who told it to you?

With a little prompting from me, we offered our recollections in response to the questions. The stories we told (stories about stories) were by turns intriguing, poignant, funny and evocative. But, when I sat down later to analyse what we had said, the results surprised me. I had been expecting early memories of being read or even told bed-time stories by parents and grandparents, perhaps even some of the traditional oral nursery rhymes and classic children's stories but what emerged was very different.

About half the group spoke about stories that had been told within their families, stories that had something to do with their place in the world. Some of these focused on close family relationships and others linked to wider social issues (such as war, class and race) or to nationality and landscape. In their different ways, both these types of story seemed to be about confirming collective identity, about belonging. They provided answers to such tacit questions as "Where do I come from? To what tribe do I owe allegiance? Who are we?" I can use some anonymous snippets to illustrate my point. Each quotation comes from a different speaker.

I thought about the time my grandmother told me about how she met my grandfather, about how she saw him standing with no shoes on at a street corner in the East End of London and thinking " that's the man I'm going to marry".

I was told stories by my grandmother and my mum, really bizarre ones, which were more about control than about stories. We had this big round table in our dining room and when I was a kid I used to be a bit hyperactive and just run round and round it and my mum would say to me, "You can't run around the table on a Sunday." My grandmother would say, "You're creating lots of dust here and you can't create dust." Then suddenly I realized that all those stories at home were told in my native tongue, Punjabi, and when I went to school all the stories and other stuff would be in English.

I thought about going to stay with my great-aunt - who was like my granny because she brought my mum up - and she'd do things with me that she did with my mum like tie my hair in rags to make ringlets. And as she was doing that she'd tell me about my mum... stories about my mum when she was a child like me.

My grandfather used to tell stories, like story-history. At first I thought it was real history and then I realized that they were lots of his stories. I remember him sitting down without his teeth in the middle of the night and wearing this great big nightshirt and launching into a story.

I was brought up on stories about the Second World War, and about living in London during the war, about how I was born, and in the hospital and so on. It was almost like being marinated in that set of stories. That war and that set of stories was part of my life in some senses, even though I was very young.

I grew up in the bush in Australia and I can't remember anyone ever talking about the past. About 15 or 20 years ago one of my aunts was seriously hooked on genealogy and she sent me a bunch of computer printouts tracing part of my family back to 1792. They were transported out to Australia as convicts and suddenly I had a past and there was a story behind me.

The other half of the group spoke about how important written stories - in comics and books - had been to them as children. They named particular stories and characters that had fascinated them, ones that had offered them fictional role models with which they could identify. The stories they told seemed to have more to do with imagining their own individual identity than with belonging. They provided answers to such tacit questions as: "How am I different from the rest of my tribe?", "Who else do I want to I be like?", "What other life can I imagine myself leading?" Again, I can illustrate my point with some anonymous quotations from different speakers.

The first stories that I remember were Marvel Comics. I think it was themes about saving the world and something about being heroic and good triumphing over evil. It was a lot about that stuff that really captured me. It took quite a long time for me to realize that the world isn't actually like that.

As a child I was sent away from home a lot to live with grandparents and to go to school and reading was a big comfort to me. The people that I liked most in books were always loners or people who themselves were slightly out of the mainstream and who did something surprising, which was absolutely brilliant and everybody loved them.

When you asked about our childhood and stories, I couldn't remember being told stories at all, so it was very much through books. I loved Enid Blyton books; they were always fairly solid sort of adventure stories. The Famous Five was a particular favourite for me... I liked to think that I was the sixth!

I immediately thought of Enid Blyton's books, which I read avidly for years and years and years. The Secret Garden by Francis Hodgson Burnett was probably my favourite story. And I loved Arthur Ransome's stories, especially Swallows and Amazons because I lived near where they are set in the Lake District. I used to absolutely lose myself in these books.

My recollection of encountering stories as a child also falls into this second category. This is what I said to the group in response to my own question.

I spent a lot of my childhood on my own, away from my mother and sister and I dived into books. I've got a book here - it's the one thing I still have from my childhood. It's called Stuart Little *by EB White. It's about a strange child, a mouse who is born to human parents. He falls in love with a bird, a beautiful bird called Margalo who flies away. Most of the book is about his search for her. I love the last few lines: "Stuart... climbed into his car and started up the road that led towards the north... As he peered ahead into the great land that stretched before him, the way seemed long. But the sky was bright, and he somehow felt he was headed in the right direction."*

I am struck by how powerfully Stuart Little's story reflected what I had felt like when growing up: that I was somehow out of place, a special child searching for someone I had lost. In my case, it had been my father who died when I was four years old. Looking back, I can see how the image of Stuart Little, heading north in his car, not knowing if he would ever find Margalo but still travelling with hope, sustained me as a child.

The extracts that I have quoted were the most graphic, but at the heart of every speaker's tale was the issue of either individual or collective identity (how am I different from, or similar to, other members of my "tribe"). Psychologist David Bakan speaks of these two issues as *agency* and *communion*, calling them the "two fundamental modalities in the existence of living forms."[11] Though the balance between these sometimes opposing forces varies in each of us, we are all motivated by both to some extent: agency leads to a desire for autonomy, power and achievement; communion to a desire for love, intimacy and social connection. Our identities are formed by the unique ways in which we enact this basic polarity and by the *self-stories* that shape our understanding of who we are.

The question of how we come to know who we are is so fundamental to understanding the human condition that it has been studied extensively in many fields: psychology, psychotherapy, philosophy, sociology, theology, linguistics, and literary criticism to name but a few. The literature is vast but tucked away in the corners of this huge virtual library is a handful of gems for the curious storyteller.

Some of these gems are to be found in the work of cognitive

psychologist Jerome Bruner[12] who developed the notion that we have two distinct modes of thought, which he called the logico-rational (or paradigmatic) mode and the narrative (or storied) mode. The former reaches for abstraction and generalisable conclusions and generates good science whilst the latter delves for the particularities of human experience and is hungry for good stories. From a lifetime of study, he concluded that our sense of self resides in a kind of internal autobiography, created and undergoing constant revision by our narrative minds.

This idea that we construct our self-identity from stories challenges the popular notion that our real identity is something essential and immutable, a kind of pre-existing authentic self that we can discover by stripping away the accumulated layers of misconceptions. Instead, says our second thinker, Donald Polkinghorne, reflecting on human existence and narrative in a seminal book, *Narrative Knowing and the Social Sciences*:

> We achieve our personal identities and self-concept through the use of narrative configuration, and make our existence into a whole by understanding it as an expression of a single unfolding and developing story. We are in the middle of our stories and cannot be sure how they will end; we are constantly having to revise the plot as new events are added to our lives.[13]

The self then is a kind of telling, but who is telling what and to whom? A third writer William Lowell Randall in *The Stories We Are*[14] suggests a way of thinking about this that storytellers may find useful when looking for ways of working with biographical and autobiographical material. He speaks about *existence* as being the sum total of the undifferentiated flow of everything that happens to us in our lives; he calls this the *outside story*. From these raw events, we consciously and unconsciously select events that have significance for us and shape them into internal narratives; these are what constitute our *experience* which he calls the *inside story*.

We convey some of our experiences to other people in the form of stories and anecdotes and the way in which we are heard may reinforce or change how we think about ourselves; he calls this *expression* or the *inside-out story*. Finally, our sense of self is influenced by the way others see us and talk about us (the stories that are told about us); here we are dealing with *impression* or the *outside-in story*.

To recapitulate Randall's view, *existence* is external and largely un-storied. *Experience* is an internal phenomenon, populated and given form by tacit, unspoken stories. *Expression* and *impression* are manifested in explicit storytelling to others and by others. This way of conceptualising the storied or narrative self provides us as storytellers with several avenues through which we can help people develop a more creative and generative relationship with their own lives. We can, for example, tell them or introduce them to a story that adds richness and diversity to their lives; we can invite them to think about the events of their lives in new ways that enrich their inner dialogue and story-making capacity; we can help them give voice to their experience in evocative and memorable stories that honour their own lives; we can support them in hearing and making sense of the stories that other people have about them.

Theologian John Dunne[15] suggests that it is through storytelling that we form our relationship to our own lives. "What kind of story are we in?" he asks. "Is it the story of an adventure, a journey, a voyage of discovery? Or is it something simpler like the story of a child playing by the sea? [For]... the human thing is not merely to live, to act, to love. It is to have a relationship to one's life, one's action, one's love..." Put another way: we imagine ourselves to be living out a story of some kind and the kind of story we imagine will shape the way we live our lives. The stories we tell are fateful. It's a sobering thought.

However we choose to look at it, self and story are deeply entwined. That was the truth that I stumbled into at Hawkwood telling *The Man Who Lived as a King* and that my colleagues and I touched upon in the storytelling workshop at

Bath. There is an old story that hints at the same truth.

A pilgrim once visited a famous guru to ask a question of existential urgency, namely:
"What supports this world on which we stand?"
"The great sea turtle supports the earth," the guru replied.
"And what supports the great sea turtle?" the anxious pilgrim inquired.
"It is the great sky turtle."
"And what supports the great sky turtle?"
"It is the great galactic turtle."
"And what supports the…."
The guru cut him off with a bored wave of the hand. "Don't bother, it's turtles all the way down."

So too with stories.

7
Storied Lives

Shamanic practitioner and storyteller Michael Berman asserts that there are significant parallels between these two roles. It is a provocative and interesting proposition, one that we can learn from without necessarily having to accept as being true. This is the nub of his argument:

> *Like the shaman, the storyteller is a walker between the worlds, a mediator between our known world and that of the unknown - someone who communes with dragons and elves, with fairies and angels, with magical and mythical beasts, with gods and goddesses, heroes and demons, able to pass freely from this world into non-ordinary reality and to help us experience those other realms for ourselves.*[16]

Certainly, as storytellers we have to take the invisible world seriously. We do not have to believe the stories we tell but unless we believe *in* them, we cannot hope to engage our listeners in anything but the most superficial manner. As we become familiar with the canon of traditional stories, we come to understand that some of them, particularly fairy stories and wonder tales, are the carriers of centuries of accumulated folk wisdom. Their meanings and messages are subtle and various. It is a serious error to ascribe a single meaning to any such story, for each telling is unique and the needs of every listener are different.

Many books have been written offering psychological interpretations of traditional stories. The best of them (such as Bruno Bettelheim's *The Uses of Enchantment* from a Freudian perspective and Marie-Louise von Franz's *The Interpretation of Fairy Tales* from a Jungian point of view), provide fascinating insights. Freudian psychoanalysis and Jungian analytic psychology both draw heavily on ancient myths to describe and explain the roots of human behaviour, as though these universal stories are imprinted on our minds at birth. That may be so but good storytellers know better than to impose their own meaning on the stories they tell. Our task is rather to tell stories in such a way that our listeners have the chance to make their own sense of them so they can take from each tale what they most need to hear.

Here, perhaps, is where the shaman (and that contemporary shaman, the psychotherapist) and the storyteller part company: the former makes use of story in a forensic way to achieve particular outcomes for their clients while the latter invites his or her listeners into the world of story so that they can make their own way towards whatever healing they are ready and able to find. I make this distinction in order to claim some legitimate ground from which storytellers can use the tremendous healing potential of storytelling without mistaking or confusing their role with that of the trained therapist. What we storytellers offer through the exercise of our craft is not therapy but it can be very therapeutic.

As I intimated in the previous chapter - when speaking of the healing possibilities of storytelling in response to William Lowell Randall's ideas of the four aspects of the storied self: existence, experience, expression and impression – sometimes the best use of our storytelling skills and hard-won understanding of how story works is to help other people tell their own stories and to hear them told in a different light. I had the chance to learn something about this way of working with story over a ten year period of running half-day storytelling workshops for mature students at the University of Bath. We used a process by which they told real-life stories that were then taken away by their colleagues, embellished and told back to them as fables or fairytales.

As you might imagine, the logistics of getting up to twenty-four people simultaneously involved in telling three rounds of stories (and the whole process repeated three times over) are somewhat complicated. Suffice it to say that during the whole process each person gets the chance to tell his or her anecdote, lift an anecdote into story form, and to tell (and receive) a fable or fairy story.

The transformation of language and imagery from round to round in these workshops was often quite remarkable. For example, a fragment from an original anecdote "I was quite successful in my early career but I knew that something was missing", became "There was a young woman who had what everyone else would see as all the trappings of success" when retold in the second round, and then appeared in the fairy story in the final round as "Once upon a time there was a golden princess who was the envy of the world. No-one but she knew that her heart was breaking."

Equally apparent at the time but more difficult to convey is the difference in the emotional and energetic qualities of each round. The telling of anecdotes from life was typified by nervous laughter and a hushed conversational tone described by one observer as reminiscent of a hospital waiting room. During the second round as these anecdotes were lifted into story form and retold in new groups, there would usually be a noticeable increase in volume in the room and much greater animation of vocal tone. In the third round, as these stories were transformed into fairy tales and told back to the people who had told the original anecdotes from which the fairy stories were derived, there would be many extravagant gestures, the sound of excited voices, rapt attention to the tales, lots of raucous laughter and not a few tears. Finally as the recipients pondered the fairy stories they had received in response to their original anecdotes, the vocal tones in the groups were typically warm and appreciative, interspersed with periods of thoughtful silence.

The detail of what was happening in the workshops was not apparent at the time, as there was too much to make sense of in the moment but clearly something interesting was going on. The real value of this process emerged later as participants reflected and wrote about their experiences. From this, I discovered over the years that many of the participants had found hidden gifts in the mythic versions of their own stories.

Here is one outstanding example that a student (let us call her Rachel) wrote about in her final dissertation. A few years before this, Rachel had suffered a cycling accident, which had caused serious physical injury and damage to her brain and it was this story that she had told to her group. Here, in her own words, is the fairy story she received in response to her anecdote:

Once upon a time there was a beautiful princess who lived in a castle in the far North. Here she studied many books of alchemy and the dark arts, and she was famed throughout the land for her wisdom and learning. Also she loved to ride out often across the hills and dales on a white horse, which she rode like the wind and with great daring.

One day, she was galloping through the forest when suddenly a hideous dwarf stepped out from behind a tree and this so frightened her horse that it tripped and fell. The princess flew through the air and hit her face so hard against an oak tree that she was never to look the same again. And when she recovered consciousness she could no longer remember who she was, or anything that had happened to her in the last five years.

But with the loving nursing of her friends she gradually recovered, so that in time she remembered once more who she was, and at last she was well enough to get on her white horse again. Then she rode far to the south, and there she found another castle, where she began to study a new white magic, and leave behind those dark arts she had learnt before. But no one knows how this story ends.

Later, she reflected:

Hearing my story told back to me as a fairy story in the words of another made it seem lighter, with a positive yet open ending for which I have to take responsibility and in this it became a tale of recovery rather than decline, and set the future course of my personal narrative.[17]

Another student (I will call her Carrie) told a story about how stuck and dissatisfied she felt in her current position at work. Later she told me that the process had encouraged her to take responsibility for changing her circumstances. In fact she continued working for the same company but doing different work that was more in keeping with her values and in another country. Here is part of the fairy story she received:

There once was a fair maiden, a free spirit with long hair, blowing freely in the wind. She was happy as she travelled far and wide to many different lands doing good work with the people from these lands. She now found herself trapped and unhappy. She wore her hair in tight braids and yearned for the day she would wear her hair free and she would be happy again.

She told me:

It was a very good way of looking at my life as a story that has been influenced by my situation, experience and others. It helped me understand and make sense of what I was experiencing at that time as a young woman, working for sustainability, in a large organisation. My key learning was that I needed to change something in my life and my current work situation - that it wasn't just me, but the situation I was in. After deciding to take the position in South America I have had a number of people tell me that they see something different about me - that I seem more alive and happy. It is that my spirit is happy and free, for the first time since I joined the company.[18]

Drawing directly from these two examples and thinking about the experience of facilitating this process on many occasions, several points are worth making about what enables it to provide such a powerful and potentially healing experience. The first point is the rather obvious one that the exercise involved an oral exchange - telling and listening rather than writing and reading. The sounded word has particular power: Walter Ong says that orally based thought and expression is "close to the human lifeworld... agonistically toned.... empathetic and participatory rather than objectively distanced, and situational rather than abstract"[19]. The storytelling exercise was deliberately structured to rely on the spoken word precisely in order to open up the possibility of stimulating these characteristically oral psycho-dynamics.

The second point is that people gave their stories away and got them back heightened and embellished. For a short time at least, they witnessed their stories move outside their control. The stories were temporarily released from the unconscious grip of the originator and given a chance to find more generative forms at the hands of other tellers. The exercise gave participants the possibility of a direct experiential understanding that their current *self-story* was only one possible construction among many. Whilst this realisation might be initially daunting, it can also be empowering. It also seems clear that having one's life stories heard with respect and returned with interest contributed to people's sense of self-worth and that the reciprocity involved in the storytelling exercise provided opportunities for deepening connections between members of the group.

Thirdly, the exercise demonstrates the imaginative power of stories to endow experience with meaning by enabling the transformation of everyday anecdotes (what the novelist James Joyce called "epiphanies of the ordinary") into fables and fairy tales in which the plight and consciousness of the characters are given archetypal forms. As a result, some participants such as Rachel and Carrie came to a new understanding of the possibilities of their situation. The shift from the mundane to the mythic, which is a particular feature of the storytelling exercise, offered participants something beyond the telling and hearing of personal stories. Mythology and psychology, it seems, are closely entwined. When we tell or hear the stories of our lives in mythic terms, we can better relate our particular individual stories to the "all human" story of everyman and everywoman.

Finally, the storytelling exercise confirms that the kind of healing offered by storytelling has to do with wholeness.

It is about working to make sense of our lives in a way that includes both the shadow and the light, thus creating and recreating an ever larger sense of self. It is about refreshing and renewing our stories to incorporate our lived experience. If our stories become fixed then we too may become rigid, defending ourselves against anything that contradicts our carefully constructed identity. If our stories fall apart or are too fluid, we may lack any coherent sense of self at all and find ourselves overly shaped by others, lacking agency and self-esteem.

Our lives *are* stories. If we do not take our life stories seriously then we diminish ourselves and if we do not take other people's life stories seriously then we diminish them. As Erving Polster, a canny old Gestalt practitioner, says in the title of his book: *Every Person's Life is Worth a Novel*. And as he concludes:

> *People often summarise the events of their lives in a word or two and then forget what it is they have summarised. At first, the special titles they give themselves are convenient symbols or guides in an otherwise incomprehensible existence. But the details, the substance of life, may be lost. When the story is told again and substance and title reconnected, congruence is restored and a sense of wholeness regained.*[20]

Witnessing dozens of people share their stories in this exercise over the years confirmed what I already believed to be the case, that storytelling is a natural human activity. It has shown itself to be so intrinsic to our humanity that I sometimes wonder if we should call ourselves *homo fabula* rather than *homo sapiens*. Indeed, I once heard that, somewhere in the world, there is an indigenous people whose name for human being, when literally translated, is "featherless story-telling creature".

Despite frequent initial protestations to the contrary, I have never found anyone who cannot, with a little encouragement and support, tell a tale.

8
Living Stories

The previous chapter explored the healing power of transforming our real-life stories into the mythic form of a fairy tale. But what about the potential of working with the opposite vector: using mythic stories to cast a healing light on our everyday stories? That might simply involve telling a particular story in performance and letting it do its work subliminally but it could also be done in a workshop setting giving more time for people to explore their connections with a story in depth. Either way, the first thing is to find a good story!

Finding the right story (one that has the richness, depth and relevance to resonate with all the participants) is crucial to the process and can be quite a challenge. It also has to be right for you, the storyteller. Unless the story grabs you viscerally and turns you upside-down, unless it speaks to you about something you may not understand but know is important for you, it just isn't going to work. Most of the storytellers that I know spend hours trawling through books, searching for stories. They also say that the best stories seem to find them in unexpected ways. The detective skills required are less like those of the laser-brained Sherlock Holmes and more like those of the bumbling 1970s and 80s television cop Lieutenant Colombo who wandered through each episode asking seemingly random questions until the identity of the perpetrator of that week's heinous crime became obvious.

A few years ago, my colleague Sue Hollingsworth and I were due to lead a four-day long workshop together at Emerson College, and I was hunting for a story. Our plan was to tell the story in several parts through the workshop and to use it as a springboard for the participants to explore whatever issues it brought up. It was not to be a therapy workshop but we hoped that it might offer the prospect of some healing.

Six weeks to go and we still had not found the right story. I had already spent many hours systematically researching our theme, scouring my books, scanning a hundred stories to no avail. Time was running out and I was getting distinctly nervous. No story, no workshop. I called Sue who was much more relaxed. "It will come," she said. "If you wait and trust, then the right story will come." A few days later, in my partner's house, I noticed an old book of Norse folktales lying on the bedside table. I picked it up and opened it at the table of contents. The title of one story immediately caught my eye: *The Giant with No Heart in His Body.* What an amazing metaphor for so many of the organisations people work in, I thought, and I immediately turned to the story.

On first reading, this centuries-old story felt just right. There were issues of the domestic and the wild, of trust and betrayal, of people being turned to stone and brought back to life, of masculine and feminine, of love and the hidden heart. There was something that touched me deeply in the image of the giant, fearfully keeping his heart hidden away from the princess only to reveal its whereabouts too late to win her love or to escape his fate. I sensed the echoes of this theme in my own life and realised that there was much this story could teach me.

As I jotted down some initial thoughts about the story in my notebook, I came across a quotation from the American mystic and group leader Richard Moss I had written down some months before:

Australian Aboriginals say that the big stories - the stories worth telling and retelling, the ones in which you may find the meaning of your life - are forever stalking the right teller, sniffing and tracking like predators hunting their prey in the bush.[21]

Maybe this story has been hunting me, I thought. The hairs on the back of my neck stood up and even though it was now late at night I sent Sue an excited text message. "Got it!"

When it came to the workshop that was the story we told. It is a Norse wonder tale[22] collected in the nineteenth century but with its origins in a centuries old oral tradition, told and retold and distilled into its essential form through a collective folk wisdom.

Once upon a time there was a king who had seven sons, and he loved them so much that he could never bear to be apart from them all at once. When they were grown up, the six eldest set off to find themselves brides. The king kept the youngest at home and told the others to bring back a princess for him too. The six brothers went off dressed in the finest clothes and riding the finest horses that money could buy. At last they came to a king who had six daughters; they fell head over heels in love with each other and soon six marriages were celebrated. After a while they set off to bring their brides home, quite forgetting to bring back a bride for Boots, their youngest brother. On the way, they passed a huge wooden door set into a steep hillside where unknown to them a giant lived. The giant came out of his house and turned them all to stone.

We told the group how Boots had eventually persuaded his father to let him go off to search for his brothers and how he had helped an injured raven, a stranded salmon and a starving wolf. The wolf, named Greylegs, took Boots to where the giant lived and told him that he could only defeat the giant, who had no heart in his body, if he listened carefully to the princess who also lived there. The princess and Boots fell in love at first sight and she formed a plan to trick the giant into revealing where he kept his hidden heart. Pretending that she loved the giant, the princess strewed wild flowers on the floor and decked out the cupboard (where the previous day he had falsely told her that he kept his heart) with scented garlands.

"And, pray, what's the meaning of all this tomfoolery?" asked the giant. "Oh, I'm so fond of you, I couldn't help doing it when I knew that your heart lay there," said the princess. "How could you be so silly as to believe any such thing?" said the giant. "How can I help believing it, when you tell me? I so want to know where your heart really lies," said the princess. "Well, if you must know, I will tell you," said the giant. "Far, far away in a lake lies an island, on that island stands a church, in that church is a well, in that well swims a duck, in that duck there is an egg, and in that lies my heart... you darling woman."

As I told that part of the story, I stumbled over the words "you darling woman", choking them back to an inaudible whisper, and had to repeat them at the request of the audience. Those were the final words of that part of the story and as Sue led the group into an exercise about the first meeting between Boots and the princess I had time to think. What had caught me in that moment?

I remembered that when I first encountered the story I had been struck by the image of the princess strewing flowers across the doorsill and hanging garlands of flowers on the cupboard where the giant had told her he kept his heart hidden. I had found something ineffably poignant about this offering (or perhaps sacrifice) of nature's beauty to the unfeeling giant, and something searingly sad about the giant's eventual and fatal capitulation to her entreaties to reveal its hiding place. "You darling woman" he calls her. These are the only words of affection he utters in the whole story: a half-mute, stumbling attempt to express a love he has been unable to embody. By then it is too late to make any difference, his fate is sealed.

This felt like familiar territory to me. I knew that I too had demanded love but withheld my own heart. I too appeared strong but was sometimes terrified of my own fragility. I too had a choice to make, right then in my life, about living more wholeheartedly, risking my heart in loving others and myself. Maybe this was why the story had found me and demanded that I tell it?

The next day, Sue and I returned to telling the story. We told the group how after travelling for many days, Boots had come to the shore of the lake and with the help of Greylegs, the raven and the salmon, crossed to the island to retrieve the duck egg from the bottom of the well. Squeezing the egg, Boots had forced the giant to bring his brothers and their brides back to life. Then, resolutely, he broke the egg into pieces and the giant burst at once.

Now he had made an end of the giant, Boots rode back again on the wolf to the giant's house, and there stood all of his six brothers, alive and merry, with their brides. Then Boots went into the hills in search of his bride and when he had found her, they all set off home again to their father's house. And you can imagine how glad the old king was when he saw all his seven sons come back, each with his bride.

When the story had ended, Sue and I invited the participants to cluster around the moments and themes in the story that had most interested them. After a short discussion each group was asked to present an improvised scene representing something about how that part of the story connected with their own lives. There were four presentations, funny and serious, touching different parts of the story: the six brothers and their brides being turned to stone; Boots setting out to search for his brothers; the wolf eating the horse; the princess strewing flowers. Finally, the last group to go, Lucy, Angela, Wallace and Nancy[23] came forward towards the small stage area to show their response to finding themselves at the point of the story where the princess is strewing flowers.

Angela stood on a chair facing the audience with a vacant expression and began to speak about organising bus routes and moving people from place to place. Her voice was flat and emotionless. She gestured with her hands but stared over our heads. After a minute or so Wallace, Nancy and Lucy entered the stage silently. They knelt and laid wild flowers on the ground round a candle. One of them lit the candle then they stood, looked at each other and held hands. Hands were extended towards Angela and she grasped them and stepped down from the chair. She stopped talking. This was all done slowly and with intense gazing at each other. I could see that both Lucy and Wallace were shaking slightly and their eyes were damp with tears.

The whole improvisation had taken several minutes. I was very moved by this scene, which seemed to be touched with the same poignancy and sadness that I had experienced when first reading the story. In this version however, the strewing of the flowers had been an act of compassion rather than one of betrayal. The giant had reclaimed his heart and his humanity. He had given up his grandiosity and power, revealing another facet of the story, one of love, forgiveness and redemption. I felt that day (and still feel now) a renewal of hope and encouragement to open my heart.

Wallace and Lucy have subsequently written accounts of their experience of this improvised response to the story. Lucy relates that Wallace told the members of their quartet that he had been working on post-conflict reconstruction in Bosnia and that he was struggling to deal with the "terrible, terrible stories" of suffering that he had encountered there. One story in particular had stuck in his mind, that of a woman who had been imprisoned and as a result of camp life had subsequently miscarried or lost babies very young five times. How could he deal with his professional life of "just going and doing the reconstruction" in the face of such horror? He and his group had decided to improvise a scene incorporating both the mundane practicalities of reconstruction and an act honouring the dead children. In his account, written several weeks after the event, Wallace reflected:

> Our planning for the tableau was brief in the extreme, and as it unfolded a voice was shouting in my head "No, no. That's not my story!" and as that attachment to "my" story faded, I feel that the power of the story grew in inverse proportion to my "ownership" of it. And of course it was exactly as it should be - the story was so powerful because the actors were presenting their truth not mine. At

this distance in time, I make a connection with the Flowers of the Forest and the poppies of Flanders. There are so many more similar stories. Will we ever learn? I feel so powerless, yet I know that what I am doing is important. That is why strewing the flowers on the giant's threshold is so important. It is the corollary of Pastor Neimüller's thought that all that is necessary for evil to triumph is for good men to do nothing. Now I know what the meaning of the giant's story was for me and why the flower-strewing was significant.

Wallace's observation, that the power of the story grew in inverse proportion to his attachment and "ownership" of it, is particularly striking. There seems to be enormous power in letting our stories go and receiving them back transfigured through the creative imagination of others. In this way, the process of meaning-making can extend beyond the original teller of the story and be reconstructed in the bodies, minds and responses of the listeners. In this case, the collective improvisation also acted as a vehicle for the emergence of multiple meanings in the actors and spectators. There was a reciprocal flow of meaning between individual and collective intelligences, in and out, back and forth, at both conscious and unconscious levels, an activation of deep eddies and currents in the sea of stories and a sense of profound healing.

We might also call it a movement of the soul. By *soul* I mean (without any religious connotation) the part of us that seeks our unique and particular form of wholeness: the oak tree latent in the acorn; the universal animating principle of being and becoming in which we all, human and non-human, partake. A story like *The Giant with No Heart in His Body* speaks the language of the soul, which understands that kings and queens, princes and princesses, horses, ravens, salmon, wolves, giants, lakes, islands, churches, wells, ducks, eggs and the hidden heart are all aspects of our selves. Working with such a story, opening the story up, enacting and embodying our responses, can implicitly help us connect with what our souls want for us, which is to become whole, to heal.

The Giant with No Heart in His Body

Once upon a time there was a king who had seven sons, and he loved them so much that he could never bear to be apart from them all at once. His wife had died young and it fell to him to bring them up alone. When they grew into young men they said to their father, "It is time for us to be married. This kingdom is small. We must go into the wide world and find ourselves brides."

The king said, "My dear sons, how could I live without you by my side? I cannot possibly let you go." But his sons protested and eventually the king agreed. "You may all go, except you Boots for you are still too young. You shall stay by my side and comfort me." Nothing Boots could say would change his father's mind and he looked on as preparations were made for the journey. The six eldest brothers were decked out in new clothes of finely woven silk and wool with fur cloaks to keep out the cold. Grooms brought the six finest horses from the royal stables and placed hand-tooled leather saddles on their backs. Servants dragged chests from the royal treasury and filled the saddle bags with dowries of gold and silver.

How splendid the six brothers looked as they set off on the high road to adventure, the old king with Boots by his side waving goodbye from the battlements. "Farewell my sons," cried the king. "Take good care of each other - and remember to bring back a bride for Boots."

They travelled far and visited many lands until, one day, they found themselves in a kingdom where the king and queen had six daughters and they fell head over heels in love; a princess for each prince and for each prince, a princess. Soon six marriages were celebrated and after six long honeymoons, the brothers set off to bring their brides home, quite forgetting to bring back a bride for Boots. The whole party rode together, laughing and singing, without a care in the world, paying little heed to their surroundings until, after several days, they came into a wooded valley with a huge, iron-studded door set into the hillside. Not a bird sang, not a creature moved, not a leaf rustled. It was so eerie and still that they too fell silent. As they crept past the door it suddenly flew open and out strode a giant, twice the height of any man.

Before they could say anything, the giant flashed his eyes and turned them all to stone then went back into his house and slammed the door shut behind him. The sound echoed like a thunderclap through the valley. A thick mist rolled down the hillside and engulfed the motionless figures of the six brothers and their brides and all their horses, standing among the trees like so many statues.

Time passed.

Meanwhile, the old king grew sadder and sadder waiting for his six sons to return home. "If you were not here," he said to Boots, "I think I would die from sorrow." "Well, father," said Boots, "I am sorry that you say so because I was thinking that I should go and look for them." He begged his father for so long that eventually he was forced to let him go. "Very well," said the king, "you have my blessing. But I'm afraid there is no money left in the treasury for fine clothes or a fine horse like your brothers had." Boots did not care about that. He put some bread and cheese into his knapsack, saddled up the last horse in the stables - a broken-winded, pot-bellied, old nag - said farewell to his father and set off on the high road to adventure.

Boots had no idea where his brothers were to be found so whenever he came to a crossroads, one way was as good as another. Soon he had wandered off the highway and onto the byways that criss-crossed the land. After a while he came across a raven lying in the road, dragging its wings, unable to fly. As he drew close, the raven looked up at him and spoke.

"Dear friend, give me some food, and I'll help you when you most need help." "I haven't much," said Boots, "but I can spare you a little. I see you need it." He took out what was left of the bread and cheese, broke it in two and gave half to the raven to eat. Soon the raven flapped his wings and took to the air, flying around in three great circles until he became just a speck in the sky and disappeared.

When he had gone a bit farther, Boots came to a brook where a great salmon thrashed around, stranded on a sandbank. As he drew close, the salmon looked up at him and spoke. "Dear friend, put me into the water again, and I'll help you when you most need help." "Well," said Boots, "I cannot see how you will be able to help me but it is a pity you should lie there and choke." He got off his horse and carefully lifted the fish into the brook. Soon the salmon swam away, the silver gleam of his body moving far upstream until he passed out of sight.

After that Boots went a long way and met a wolf which was so famished that it crawled along the road on its belly, its coat was mangy and its eyes were dim. As he drew close, the wolf looked up at him and spoke. "Dear friend, let me have your horse. I'm so hungry the wind whistles through my ribs. I've had nothing to eat these two years." "No," said Boots, "I was happy to help the raven and the salmon but what you ask is impossible. Besides, if I gave you my horse I would have nothing to ride on." "If you help me," said the wolf, "then you can ride upon my back, and I'll help you when you most need help." "Well," said Boots, "I cannot see how you will be able to help me but you may take my horse, since you are in such need."

When the wolf had eaten the horse, he stood tall and strong once more, his coat sleek and his eyes shining bright. Boots put the bit into the wolf's jaw, and placed the saddle on him. "I am Greylegs," said the wolf. "Climb on my back and tell me where you want to go." "If only I knew," said Boots. "I am searching for my six brothers but I have no idea where they are." "I know where to find them," said Greylegs. "Hold on tight," and they set off like the wind.

Straight as an arrow went Greylegs, over hill and mountain, through river and valley, his feet scarcely touching the ground. They didn't stop for three days and three nights. On the morning of the fourth day, they came into a wooded valley with a huge, iron-studded door set into the hillside. A thick mist lay all around them; not a bird sang, not a creature moved, not a leaf rustled. Through the gloom, Boots could just make out the motionless figures of his six brothers and their brides and all their horses, standing among the trees like so many statues. Gingerly he touched their cold forms. "What has happened to them, Greylegs?"

"This is the work of the giant who lives in the hillside behind that door. If you want to free them you must go inside and face him," replied the wolf.

"But won't he turn me to stone as well? How can I possibly defeat him?" asked Boots.

"There is hope," said Greylegs. "When you get inside you'll find a princess and she'll tell you what to do to make an end of him." Leaving the wolf among the trees, Boots reached up to his full height, grasped the door handle and pushed as hard as he could. The door creaked open and Boots tiptoed alone into the giant's house. He made his way from room to room, past chairs as big as beds and tables as high as his head. There was no sign of the giant but in one of the rooms, sitting in an ordinary-sized chair, by an ordinary-sized fireplace was an ordinary-sized princess. Her golden hair hung to her waist and her bright blue eyes glinted in the firelight. She was so lovely that Boots fell in love with her at first sight. "Who are you?" she asked. "What are you doing here?"

"My name is Boots. I have come to defeat the giant and free my brothers. I'll save you too if I can." "Oh, heaven help you!" said the princess. "This will surely be the death of you. No one can kill the giant who lives here, for he has no heart in his body." "Well, now that I am here, what are we to do?" asked Boots. There must have been something about him that took her fancy because the princess replied, "The giant will be home soon. Hide under the bed as quiet as a mouse and listen carefully to everything we say." He had only just got under the bed when the door crashed open and in came the giant demanding two fat sheep for his supper. After he had eaten his fill, the giant and the princess went to bed.

After a while, the princess said, "There is one thing I would like to ask you if only I dared."

"What thing is that?" asked the giant.

"Where do you keep your heart, since you don't carry it about in your body?"

"That is none of your business," said the giant, "but, if you must know, it lies under the door-sill." He turned away from her and soon began to snore, shaking the bed like a small earthquake.

The next morning as soon as the giant left the house Boots and the princess set to work to look under the door-sill for his heart. But the more they dug, and the more they hunted, the more they couldn't find it. "He has fooled us this time," said the princess.

"We'll have to try again." So they filled the hole and carefully put back the door-sill. Then she picked all the prettiest flowers she could find, and strewed them over the door-sill. When it was time for the giant to come home, Boots hid himself again. He had only just got under the bed when the door crashed open and in came the giant with his muddy boots, each one made from a whole ox hide, tramping across the door-sill.

"What's the meaning of all these flowers?" asked the giant.

"Ah!" said the princess, "I'm so fond of you that I couldn't help strewing them, when I knew that is where you keep your heart."

"You don't say so!" laughed the giant. "You foolish girl, I don't keep it there at all."

When he had eaten a roasted goat and a whole sack of turnips for his supper, the giant and the princess went to bed. After a while, the princess asked the giant again where his heart was, for she said she would so like to know. "Well," said the giant, "if you must know, I keep it in that cupboard against the wall." He turned away from her and quickly fell fast asleep, dreaming of a mouse under his bed.

Next morning as soon as the giant was gone Boots and the princess turned everything out of the cupboard hunting for his heart: flour and sugar, salt and pepper, herbs and spices, cups and saucers, pots and pans, dishes and dustpans, but the more they looked for it, the less they found it. "Well," said the princess, "we'll just try him once more." So they carefully put everything back just as before. Then the princess strung garlands of sweet-smelling wild flowers on the cupboard and Boots crept under the bed again.

Soon the giant came home. He took off his bearskin hat and hung it on the peg by the cupboard.

"Who did this? What is the meaning of all these flowers?" roared the giant.

"I put them there," said the princess. "When you told me that is where you keep your heart, I couldn't help myself."

"How could you be so silly as to believe such a thing?" said the giant. "I don't keep my heart there at all. Now, where is my supper?"

When he had eaten his fill of roasted duck, partridge, goose, quail and pheasant, the giant and the princess went to bed. After a while, the princess said, "My dear, I so want to know where your heart lies. It would be such a comfort to me think of it safely out of harm's way."

"Well, if you really must know, I will tell you," said the giant. "Far, far away there is a lake, in the middle of the lake there is an island, standing on that island there is a church, in that church there is a deep well, swimming on the waters of that well there is a duck, inside that duck there is an egg, and inside that egg is where I keep my heart... you darling woman." He turned away from her with a rare smile upon his face and soon fell fast asleep.

Early in the morning, the giant left the house, calling out that he would be back at suppertime. "I must go too," said Boots to the princess. "I'll find the lake somehow and do my best to make an end of him. Wait for me but be careful because if I fail, he will be terribly angry."

"It is you that must take care," said the princess. "Don't worry about me."

Boots took her in his arms, kissed her farewell and left the house. When he got outside, there stood Greylegs, waiting patiently in the misty wood. "Climb on my back and tell me where you want to go." So Boots told him everything that had happened inside the house, and that he must somehow find the well in the church. "I know where to find it," said Greylegs. "Hold on tight," and they set off like the wind.

Straight as an arrow went Greylegs, over hill and mountain, through river and valley, his feet scarcely touching the ground. They didn't stop for three days and three nights. On the morning of the fourth day, they came to the edge of a wide lake. Far out, in the very centre, was an island and on it Boots could just make out a church spire. "We're here, Greylegs. But I cannot swim. We've come so far together; what am I to do?"

"You may not be able to swim, but I can. I promised to help you when you most needed help. Hold on tight and don't be afraid," said Greylegs.

Boots leaned forward in the saddle and clung to the thick fur of the wolf's neck. Greylegs slipped into the cold, dark water and swam out to the island as easily and smoothly as if he had webbed feet and his rider had been no heavier than a feather on his back. Once they reached the shore, Boots got down and walked beside

Greylegs to the church. Cobwebs hung from the dusty windows and the crumbling stone arch above the door. All was silent and still as though no-one had been there for a hundred years or more. Boots reached out to turn the door handle but it was locked. There must be a key somewhere. He looked on window ledges, he looked under stones, he looked on the ground and, finally, he looked up. There, hanging from a hook at the very top of the spire, was a key.

"That must be it, Greylegs. But I cannot climb the spire. We've come so far together; what am I to do?"

"I cannot help you reach the key," said Greylegs. "But there may be one who can. Now is the time to call on the raven." So Boots put his fingers in his mouth and whistled. Soon a black speck appeared in the sky and circled round three times, closer and closer. The raven plucked the key from the hook and swooped down to place it on the ground by the door. Boots thanked the raven then took the key and fitted it to the lock. The door swung open and there in front of them was a well and on the water of the well, just as the giant had said, swam a duck.

Boots called and coaxed the duck until it came within his reach. Then he grabbed it in both arms and pulled it, squawking and quacking, towards his chest. But just as he lifted the duck up, it dropped the egg into the water and down, down, down it went, to the very bottom of the well.

"Now we've lost it, Greylegs. I cannot dive to fetch the egg. We've come so far together; what am I to do?"

"I cannot help you fetch the egg," said Greylegs. "But there may be one who can. Now is the time to call on the salmon." So Boots put his face close to the water and called his name. Soon he saw a silver gleam in the depths of the well coming closer and closer until the head of the salmon broke the surface of the water carrying the duck egg in its mouth. Boots thanked the salmon, reached out and took the egg in both hands. It was warm and pulsed softly. "Now, squeeze it," said Greylegs.

Boots did as he had been told. The egg writhed and squirmed in his grip and from far, far away the sound of the giant's screams rolled across the lake and echoed round the dank rafters of the church.

"Again," said Greylegs. "Harder."

Boots squeezed a second time.

"Spare me," screamed the giant. "I'll do anything you want. Just don't squeeze my heart in two."

"Tell him you will spare his life if he will restore your brothers and their brides to life again," said the wolf.

Boots commanded the giant as he had been told. The giant agreed and far, far away the mist lifted and the motionless figures of the six brothers and their brides and all their horses, standing among the trees like so many statues, stirred into life.

"Now, crush the egg," said Greylegs.

Boots squeezed the giant's heart until it burst. Far, far away, with a great cry, the giant exploded into a thousand pieces. Slowly the sound faded away. The giant had disappeared and was never seen again.

Boots rode back again on the wolf to the giant's house, and there stood his golden-haired princess and all of his six brothers, alive and merry, with their brides. They hugged and kissed each other and set off home to their father's house, Greylegs leading the way.

And you can imagine how glad the old king was when he saw his seven sons come back, each with his bride. He welcomed them, one and all, with tears in his eyes and ordered the servants to prepare a great homecoming feast. That evening, once the stories of their adventures had been told and re-told, the king sat Boots and his princess at the head of the table. Then he joined their hands together as husband and wife and gave the marriage toast.

"May you live long and be happy. May your children be fair of face and kind of heart. And may none of you ever be troubled by giants again."

The laughter was both loud and long, and after the toast came the feast, such a feast as had never been seen in that land before or since. And after the feasting came the music and the dancing. They danced and danced, those brothers and their brides, and if they have not stopped, they are dancing still.

About the story

This is a Norwegian story, originally collected by Asbjørsen and Moe in the mid-nineteenth century and was first translated into English by Sir George Webbe Dasent in 1859. This version is adapted from an undated volume of Dasent's translations *Tales from the Norse*, published by Blackie and Sons Ltd, Glasgow. It follows the original quite closely apart from the removal of some archaisms.

9
Telling the Untold Story

Hidden inside every tale we tell there is a pot of gold: a wealth of untold stories. Inevitably, the main narrative focuses on a few key episodes in the lives of its heroes and heroines and we only catch glimpses of the whole cast of supporting characters who appear briefly and often disappear without trace. For every question a story answers, it poses many more. Thinking about the story told in the previous chapter, *The Giant with No Heart in His Body,* we might ask, for example: How did the old king and queen (Boots' father and mother) meet? What did the old king do when Boots left to look for his brothers? How did the raven hurt his wing, the salmon get stuck on the sandbank and Greylegs the wolf become starving? Where did the princess come from and what kind of life did she have with the giant? And so on.

The questions are endless and one could argue that they are not really relevant to the story that is being told. But these *back-stories* form part of the rich imaginal world, which the storyteller needs to have internalised in order to tell the story convincingly. What is more, the healing potential of stories is often found by looking in the unexplored nooks and crannies, by following the loose ends - the threads not spun into the tale. Sometimes our sympathies do not lie with the hero or heroine. The fate of a minor character or even the ostensible villain of the piece catches our fancy or touches us in some way.

We can choose to let such moments go but if the thought or feeling stays with you then it is a good idea to follow it up somehow. What it calls for is what Arthur Frank (writing about creating restorative narratives) refers to as *thinking with the story*:

> Not think[ing] about stories, which would be the usual phrase, but think[ing] with them. To think about a story is to reduce it to content and then analyze that content... To think with a story is to experience it affecting one's own life and to find in that effect a certain truth of one's life.[24]

How in practice can we do that? We can continue to play with the story and keep it alive and active in our bodies and imaginations in any number of ways: poetry, painting, dance, improvisation, re-telling the story, creating new stories in response to the original. We can use expressive forms that we are comfortable with or ones that we find challenging. The important thing is to follow your intuition and *think with* the parts of the story that move you or speak to you in some way.

When I came across *The Giant with No Heart in His Body* and told it with Sue Hollingsworth at Emerson College, it was the giant's fate that touched me most: betrayed at the very moment he opened his heart to the princess then tricked and dispatched by Boots and Greylegs without mercy. For several years after the workshop, I told the story regularly to different groups and recently I became consumed with a desire to know what became of the giant after his heart was burst and he disappeared from the story.

Being the age I am, the phrase "what became of the giant" put me in mind of the classic 1960s Jimmy Ruffin song: *What Becomes of the Broken Hearted?*[25] I sat down at the computer keyboard and the following story flowed onto the screen in answer to the question posed by the song title.

> Boots squeezed the giant's heart until it burst. With a great cry, the giant seemed to explode, as if into a thousand pieces. Slowly the sound faded away. The giant had disappeared and was never seen again - at least, not in that world.
>
> Much later the giant woke up. The sun was shining and he was lying on a grassy bank, surrounded by a sea of wild flowers. He

was feeling groggy and confused; his chest ached. "Where am I? How did I get here?" he wondered. He sat up slowly and put one hand on the ground to steady himself. Then he noticed something strange: the flowers were not miniscule but quite big. Big enough, he realised, for a bunch of them to make a good handful. He looked around curiously. On top of the bank, an oak tree towered above him. A pair of wood pigeons clattered and cooed in its branches - they too seemed unusually large. He saw acorns lying on the ground and picked some up. Six of them filled the palm of his hand.

Wherever he was, things were on the same scale as he was. He felt happy. It was such a relief not to feel enormous compared to everything around him. But just as he was thinking this and smiling to himself he heard a distant sound that signalled the onset of misery. It was a woman's voice, singing. "Oh no," he thought. "Just as things were going so well." Women were such mysterious creatures - so small and so easily hurt, so demanding and so hurtful when their demands were not met. Always, like a moth to a flame, he was drawn by their fragile beauty and always he got burnt. He stood behind the bole of the oak tree and looked out cautiously in the direction of the song, which seemed to be getting louder.

There she was, a tiny figure on the far side of the expanse of meadow that swept from the bank towards the horizon. She was walking quickly, coming straight towards him, singing at the top of her voice:

> I'll be searching everywhere
> Just to find someone to care
>
> I'll be looking everyday
> I know I'm going to find a way
>
> Nothing's going to stop me now
> I will find a way somehow

To his amazement, the giant found himself humming along with the tune. He was smiling. He couldn't remember the last time he had smiled. As the figure drew closer, he could see that it was that of a young woman. She was pretty - dark-haired, slender and tall - very tall, almost as tall as he was in fact. But women were small creatures; they hardly came up to his waist. She must be a giant too, he thought. He stepped out from behind the oak tree and blurted out:

"Hello. You must be a gi…"

"I'm Maria," she said, smiling. "What's your name?"

"My name? Nobody has asked me that for a long time. My name… is Gruffydd."

"Hello, Gruffydd. What are you doing here?"

"I don't know. I just woke up here." He looked at the young woman, in wonder. "You're a giant like me, aren't you?"

"A giant!" Maria laughed. "What do you mean a giant? Everybody is the same size as us, more or less. I've never heard of anybody seeing a giant."

"I don't understand," said Gruffydd, rubbing his head. "I think I must have had a bad dream and my chest aches."

"That could be serious," said Maria. "Let me see if you are alright." She placed the palm of her right hand on his chest. "Does that hurt? No? That's a good sign." She dropped her hand, stepped closer and laid her head where her hand had been.

Gruffydd used all his willpower not to pull away. "What are you doing?" he said.

"Listening to your heart beating," said Maria. "It sounds good and strong to me. I wonder why it aches."

"My heart was broken," said Gruffydd, remembering the time before he woke up under the oak tree.

"Oh dear," said Maria. "That's terrible. What happened to you?"

They sat down beside each other on the grassy bank and Gruffydd began. "Where I was before, I was twice the size of everybody else. Everything moved so quickly, people and animals seemed to buzz around like insects. It made my head hurt, and that made me grumpy. But I was strong, much stronger than anyone else and so I could do things other people couldn't do. Kings and queens asked me to do things for them: kill dragons, tear down mountains, and defeat champion warriors. They rewarded me and I became rich and famous. Men said they wanted to be like me and women said that they loved me."

"That doesn't sound so bad," said Maria.

"It was alright at first but the men weren't my friends because they were frightened of me and the women didn't really love me. They didn't even like me. They just wanted my money. They would say nice things to trick me. As soon as they got what they wanted they left. It was horrible."

"Go on," said Maria.

"When I realised what those women were like, I played them at their own game. I started pretending that I loved them so that they would stay with me for a while. They said that I was heartless but I didn't let them trick me anymore."

"You were looking after yourself," said Maria.

"Well, I didn't do a very good job because one day a princess came along, a real live princess. She told me that she didn't mind that I was big and slow. She told me that she really, truly loved me. I let her live with me in my house and I thought that we were happy together. I went off questing each day, doing what the kings and queens had asked me to do and she stayed at home and looked after the place. Then, one day… " Gruffydd paused, his voice catching in his throat. Tears welled up in his eyes.

"It's alright," said Maria. "You can tell me anything. I want to know."

"One day, she asked me where I kept my heart. She put flowers all over the house. She told me that she loved me so much that it was safe to open my heart to her. I was scared but I did open my heart. I told her that I loved her too and then I joked that I kept my heart in an egg, inside a duck, swimming on a well, in a church on an island, far far away. But she was just leading me on, playing with me like all the others. She laughed at me, told me that I was huge and hideous and that she was leaving with her lover, a young man she had sneaked into our house under my nose. She broke my heart."

"You poor thing," said Maria. "No wonder your heart aches. But it's not broken. I heard it myself, it is inside your chest and it works perfectly well. Do you want to know what I think?"

Gruffydd looked at her innocent shining face, inches from his own and nodded.

"I think that wherever you have come from and whoever you met there, was just too small for you. You have a big heart and it is *wide open." Maria stood up and offered him her hand. "I'm going home now. Will you walk with me?"*

Gruffydd rose to his feet and took her hand. He could hardly believe that this delightful girl was smiling at him and inviting him to go with her. "I'd like that," he said. "Would you sing that song again, the one you were singing when you came over the meadow towards the oak tree?"

"Only if you sing it with me," said Maria. "Listen carefully and join in when you've caught the tune." She sang the first two lines and then Gruffydd joined his voice to hers.

What becomes of the broken hearted
Who had love that's now departed?

I know I've got to find
Some kind of peace of mind

I'll be searching everywhere
Just to find someone to care.

I'll be looking everyday
I know I'm going to find a way

Nothing's going to stop me now
I will find a way somehow

As they sang, they walked together hand-in-hand over the bright, sunlit meadow towards the horizon, their harmony echoing to the hills beyond.

Is it my story too? Of course it is.

Did writing it heal something in me? You bet it did.

Am I advocating that we all - storytellers and story-listeners alike - follow our own creative impulse in response to stories that move us? Absolutely.

10
Hermes in the Gorge

When our real-life stories are touched by the power of archetypal stories we sometimes experience the kind of magic that Jung called *synchronicity* - a term he coined to describe the alignment of universal forces with the life experiences of an individual, a time when things come together for us because we and they are part of a greater whole. When these moments occur in stories they profoundly affect the destinies of the characters involved. When they happen to us they can change our lives too.

If we are resolutely sceptical we can choose to dismiss such moments as mere coincidences. But storytellers cannot afford to be too sceptical. Our craft depends on imagination and the willing suspension of disbelief. Our work regularly takes us to the boundary between the visible and invisible worlds, the edge between the known and the unknown, where the human and the more-than-human meet. This is a place of enchantment, where stories weave their spells on tellers and listeners alike.

The ancient Greeks thought of these as *liminal* spaces (after *limen* for threshold) ruled by Hermes, friend to humankind, guide of souls, arch-trickster, and messenger of the gods. This kind of archetypal energy is so crucial to storytelling that if we storytellers were to petition the Olympian gods for a patron deity of our own, I like to think that Hermes would be the first to step forward.

The unexpected blessing that comes from fortuitous events (in Jung's terms, *synchronicities*) the Greeks called *hermaion* - a gift of Hermes. This chapter tells a true story about such a gift, one that brought profound insight and healing. What happened was not planned in any way; my part in it was just to tell a story (in the form of a poem). I take no personal credit for the impact on the person I told it to, I was as much caught up in the mystery as everyone else. I simply listened to the voice of Hermes and followed my storyteller's intuition.

It happened a few years ago in Crete, a wild and mountainous country, where it is said the feet of the ancient Gods once touched the earth. A small group of us from England were staying in the village of Amari as guests of our friend Stella and her husband Manolis. There were several other old friends in the group and two people, Grace and Jane, who I did not know. The week had been organised by Stella and fellow-storyteller Heleni, and included an excursion into the countryside.

"Geoff, I want you to stay at the back of the line," said Ari, our guide. "I need to know that we don't leave anyone behind."

"OK, I'll do that." I puffed up my chest a little. It felt rather good to be trusted with this responsibility.

Carefully watching our footsteps, the twelve of us set off in a slow, winding procession down the rough track. The day was hot but we were walking deep in the gorge of Patsos and protected from direct sunlight. We followed Ari along the dried up river bed, scrambling over boulders, edging along narrow paths. The air hung heavy with the scent of thyme and buzzed with insects.

People walked in twos and threes, conversations flowing and shifting throughout the day. Sometimes one or other of the group dropped back to join me for a while at the rear of the column. From time to time we all stopped and gathered around Ari as he told us about a particular plant or creature.

Once Ari called us to a halt and climbed up the side of the gorge until he was standing on a tiny ledge ten feet above our heads. He was a large man, no longer young, and his speed and agility on the rock face were astonishing. He reached out and plucked a small flower then clambered back down and held it out for our inspection.

"This one here is called *Dictamos Erondas*, it is given as a love token when it blooms. It is very beautiful but has a bad name because it only grows in the most inaccessible places and many a young man has fallen to his death trying to gather flowers for his sweetheart."

We laughed nervously at his little joke. As we moved off again, Grace pointed to a scrubby tree with dark shiny leaves, barely clinging to the rocks to our right.

"What is this bush called?" she asked.

"It is a laurel. In Greek we call it *Daphne*."

"That's amazing, Daphne is my real name. I haven't used it for years."

"Well then, Daphne," said Ari. "Let me make you a crown," and he pulled off two or three slender branches, wove them quickly into a wreath and placed it on her head.

Grace bowed graciously. "Thank you."

She smiled but I could see sadness in her eyes and she trembled slightly with some other emotion - fear, perhaps? I could not be sure and when we continued our walk her reaction stayed with me. I didn't know her well, knew nothing of her history or life story, but I began to feel something stirring in me. I wanted to give her a gift, something to acknowledge her reconnection with her given name.

Suddenly I recalled the poem that my friend Peter and I had learned the year before when we had been out sailing together. It was by Rilke, one of the *Sonnets to Orpheus*[26]. It was just about the only poem I knew by heart and it referred to Daphne, the nymph who changed herself into a laurel tree when chased by an over-amorous Apollo. I turned the words over in my mind. I hesitated: perhaps it was a bit presumptuous of me? Maybe I would forget it halfway through and look foolish. It might be better just to let it go. What did I know anyway? Who did I think I was?

Then my mind went back to what had happened a few hours before, by the cave - known locally as the cave of Hermes - at the head of the gorge, where we had told stories of the God before setting out. One of the party, Heleni, had told the story of Hermes as a baby, stealing Apollo's cattle and I had added some observations and reflections. My own words echoed round my head as I walked.

"Hermes is the god of liminal spaces, of transformation,

of crossroads, of journeys, of tricksters, thieves, market places and magic. It is Hermes who brings us messages from the Gods and it is Hermes who conducts our souls to and from the other world. He is the friendliest and most approachable of the gods. He appears when he is most needed and least expected, and offers his gifts in ways we may not immediately understand for his ways are subtle. Hermes is our companion when we take "the road less travelled by". He is always waiting to slip under our defences, willing to give us the benefit of the doubt, wanting only the best for us."

As I thought back to what I had said then, I realised that this was not about me, not about getting it right. Standing in a place so closely associated with Hermes, it occurred to me that my job was simply to deliver the message. This gift of a poem was not coming from me but through me. I could feel it rising up like a tide. I called out to Grace who was walking just ahead of me with her friend Jane.

"Grace, wait a moment. I've got something for you."

They both stopped and turned towards me. Jane put her arm around Grace's shoulders. Grace looked at me. "What is it?"

"It's a poem I think you might like to hear." We were standing no more than three feet apart. I began.

> Want the change. Be inspired by the flame
> where everything shines as it disappears.
> The artist, when sketching, loves nothing so much
> as the curve of the body as it turns away.

It was as though the world around us had stopped turning on its axis. We seemed to drop into a different dimension of time and space. I felt the words coming through me with no effort as though spoken by someone else.

> What locks itself in sameness has congealed.
> Is it safer to be gray and numb?
> What turns hard becomes rigid
> and is easily shattered.

Pour yourself out like a fountain.
Flow into the knowledge that what you are seeking
finishes often at the start, and, with ending, begins.

Now we were standing, as if naked in the presence of the poem, in the presence of some archetypal energy, perhaps in the presence of Hermes himself.

Every happiness is the child of a separation
It did not think it could survive.
And Daphne, becoming a laurel,
dares you to become the wind.

The poem ended, the world slowly began turning once more. I could feel a breeze on my cheek, and I noticed the sunlight and the shadows falling across Grace's face. I saw bright tears well up in her eyes and she sobbed gently while Jane held her.

"It just came to me," I said. "And I had to tell you."

Grace stopped crying. "You don't know how much this means to me. I came here to Crete hoping for some kind of message. I was at a workshop in Switzerland recently and somebody told me to "trust the trickster". But I had no idea what might come. I am crying because I am grateful but also because it is a tough message to hear."

The three of us hugged and laughed, before resuming our walk. Later, Grace told me that her father had named her Daphne and that she had rejected the name when he left them. "And I am at a crisis point in my own life right now. I don't know what to do but now I know that I must do something. I have to 'want the change' whatever it is. The poem was a blessing. Thank you."

I felt equally blessed for having been the vehicle for this *hermaion*, this gift of Hermes. I had no idea what crisis she was facing in her life and other than its obvious emotional impact I equally had no idea what the poem had meant to her. As I had told the group earlier, the ways of Hermes are subtle and he offers his gifts in ways we may not immediately understand.

Nevertheless, the experience had been so striking that I wrote an account of it as soon as I got back home from the holiday. I sent a copy of it to Grace, but apart from an emailed note of thanks, heard nothing more for a long time.

We bumped into each other by chance two years later and she told me how the experience had challenged, affirmed and supported her in changing her life. She also felt ready to write her own version of the experience and she promised to send me a copy. She was as good as her word: a month later I received her account. Since the storyteller's role is as much about evoking stories as telling them, here is Grace's story[27] in her own voice and her own words. Her perspective as the person who received the gift of the poem provides a valuable counterpoint to my point of view as the one who recited it. Also it was written two years later and thus gives a better sense of the enduring impact of the event.

My story begins two weeks prior to being in Crete when I was in the Swiss Alps at a Sufi summer camp where I received guidance that I was to listen for a message from the Trickster. Ehm! I thought. Trickster, what do I know about the Trickster, where am I likely to get such a message?

I had no idea but I was definitely looking for an answer to a long-term question: whether or not to leave my marriage? It seemed too good to end and not good enough to continue. I had wracked my heart and soul for a clear answer for a very long time. I knew I was very frightened to leave and step into the void. So this summer I was travelling alone, not something I would normally choose to do, but I knew I must find my own answers.

I had visited my friends in Crete previously and felt very at home there, as though it were my spiritual home in the sun. I was excited about walking the gorge; I had heard that it was quite magical and very beautiful. Before setting off to walk, we stayed a while at Hermes' cave at the entrance to the gorge. Here Geoff spoke to us of Hermes and how connected he felt with this messenger God and how helpful he had found him in times of difficulty. I realised then that of course Hermes was the arch Trickster, so listened very attentively in case there was a message for me. A good story, but no message in particular for me.

Walking the gorge was wonderful; raw nature, enormous boulders to climb over or under, high cliffs on both sides and no sign of any interference by man apart from the occasional rickety wooden bridge that blended into the landscape. I felt happy, relaxed and was enjoying every moment. It was fun when Ari crowned me with laurel, I had been aware of its connection with Daphne, a name I feel conflicted with but still use as my official name and at home in Ireland.

When Geoff called me back and told me he had something for me I was curious but in no way prepared for what was to follow. Fortunately Jane, my close friend, chose to come with me. She knows me well and as the poem unfolded, I knew that she would understand the depth of meaning it held for me.

"Want the change." Geoff had barely started and I felt the power of it. As he continued I could hardly take in the enormity of what he was saying. "What locks itself in sameness has congealed." Is that what I had done I asked myself? How awful! I do not want to be congealed. He went on. "Is it safer to be gray and numb?" By this point I was shaking. This had been written for me. I began to cry, I was feeling completely overwhelmed.

"Pour yourself out like a fountain. Flow into the knowledge of what you are seeking." How could this man I had never met before hit the nail on the head like this, how could he remember all the words, what was happening? I was clinging on to Jane. Geoff seemed to recite the sonnet effortlessly as though he had hundreds he could rattle off at will.

I couldn't take in any more words, I was overcome. This was the Trickster talking. It was as though the gods spoke directly to me. My mind was racing back to the Alps and at the same time desperately trying to hang on to what he was saying, but I couldn't. I couldn't think, or move. I had difficulty breathing. It was as though time stood still and every cell of my body was being realigned.

Then came the words, "Every happiness is the child of a separation it did not think it could survive". That completely undid me. I don't know how to describe this experience. As I write this I can feel it as though it was happening today although in fact it *was two years ago, almost to the day. I knew something profound was happening, this was a place of no return, of knowing my truth, no matter how scary. I was transfixed to the spot, marvelling at the man delivering this message, or was it the man that delivered it? I don't know. Certainly it was Geoff speaking but perhaps he was only the mouthpiece. How could he remember it word perfect without stumbling or doubting?*

Finally he ended with "And Daphne becoming a laurel dares you to become the wind." These words sounded exciting and inviting. Throughout he had held eye contact with me, while Jane held me physically. I was unable to move or speak, soft tears poured down my cheeks, it felt as though all my circuits had been blown, and that the gods themselves spoke directly to me in this ancient and beautiful gorge.

I left Crete by ferry that evening and sat on the deck watching the land disappear, astounded and in wonderment at the synchronicity of events of the previous two weeks.

I did make the change and am in the void, living my truth and feeling enlivened and excited by the change. Not knowing the future but living each moment as it arises - though not always with ease!

Healing ourselves (and helping others heal themselves) through stories is a growing field. Books on Narrative Therapy[28], Therapeutic Storymaking[29] and Biographical Counselling[30] all offer evidence of its growing importance in the therapeutic professions. My concern has been to show how we as storytellers (not as therapists) can put the knowledge and skill that comes from the practice of our craft in the service of healing. I have suggested in previous chapters that telling our own stories in mythic (and true-to-life) forms, connecting with the stories that create our self-identity (especially from childhood), having our stories transformed and told back to us as fairy stories, and exploring the tacit wisdom of wonder tales and responding to them creatively, are all potentially valuable contributions.

In this chapter, I acknowledge the mystery that lies behind storytelling - indeed behind life itself - and speak of the archetypal healing energy of Hermes that is manifested in moments of *synchronicity*. At such times, if we ourselves are open, it seems as if a door opens between the visible and invisible worlds. The stories of Gods and of men and women intermingle and nothing is ever quite the same again. Had they been transported from ancient times to stand alongside Grace, as Ari made her a crown of laurel and I recited the poem on that magical day in the gorge of Patsos, I think that our Cretan forbears would have touched their noses, looked at us knowingly and whispered a thankful prayer to Hermes.

Men & Storytelling

"Who are you really, wanderer?"
and the answer you have to give
no matter how dark and cold
the world around you is:
"Maybe I'm a king."

William Stafford

11
We Band of Brothers

This section of the book is about men and their stories, but it is not just for men. A lot has been written in recent years about masculinity in our current age, much of it rightly critical of patriarchal behaviours and some of it downright derogatory. But the question of what it means to live well as a man has received less attention and I hope that these chapters - based on personal experience - will offer valuable insights to men and women alike.

Some of those insights are about how telling stories can bring men closer together as brothers, fathers and sons. Others are about how certain kinds of story illuminate the nature of our journeys through life. All of them concern aspects of storytelling that are rarely spotlighted and demand far more from the storyteller than the exercise of his or her craft. There is something here for any storyteller who wishes to work with groups of men (or groups of women[31]) or who wants to glimpse how storytelling can help us strengthen the bonds of love between us and our parents and children.

As we become storytellers, questions inevitably arise about what sort of stories we want to tell and to whom. The possibilities are endless - a sea of stories and a host of different audiences - and such variety is part of the richness and joy of storytelling. There is no reason to restrict ourselves to any one kind of story or any single category of listener. Nevertheless, in time, we are likely to find ourselves drawn towards certain genres of story and to feel more excited by telling to particular types of audiences.

The stories we are drawn to tell are often the ones that

we most need to hear. The audiences that we best serve are generally ones which reflect some important aspects of ourselves and our lives. We may continue to relish telling different types of stories in a wide variety of settings but it is by telling the stories we love to the audiences that most attract us that we can find our home ground as storytellers and make our own unique contribution.

Early on I realised that I loved listening to and telling traditional wondertales, stories where the human and the more-than-human worlds meet, where the protagonists fall from grace and are driven to undertake demanding quests and long journeys in the course of which they learn who they truly are and how (and with whom) they are meant to spend their lives. Discovering that I had a passion for telling such stories to groups of men came later although it was prefigured by a rather strange event. Towards the end of my full-time training at the School for Storytelling a fellow student, Garth, asked "What do you want to do with your storytelling, Geoff?"

"I want to tell stories to men," I heard myself say. The words came out of my mouth unbidden. I felt a surge of energy run through my body and spontaneously I hurled my mug at the ground where it exploded into fragments like a small grenade going off. I stood there shocked and silent. "Well, that seems clear enough," said Garth and we both laughed.

I am not alone in telling stories to groups of men and I certainly was not the first to do so. Robert Bly (whose best-selling book *Iron John*[32] has influenced a generation of men in both the US and the UK) and Michael Meade (whose excellent book *Men and the Water of Life*[33] is also based on traditional stories) can lay claim to establishing and popularising the practice. Their main concern was the lack of initiation for young men into healthy masculinity in modern society and the stories they draw upon are classic heroes' journeys of the type that Joseph Campbell describes in *The Hero With a Thousand Faces*:

A hero ventures forth from the world of common day into a region of supernatural wonder: fabulous forces are there encountered and a decisive victory is won: the hero comes back from this mysterious adventure with the power to bestow boons on his fellow man. [34]

However, the notion of the hero encapsulated in such stories can only take us so far - usually to a symbolic marriage and life "happily ever after". They are stories about responding to the call of adventure, of journeying out and returning changed. By means of good luck, courage and magic, the youth overcomes all obstacles, marries his princess and becomes a king. But those of us - men and women - who have lived long enough know that "happily ever after" does not last for ever; the hero's journey is a story for the first half of life. What happens then? What is called for when good luck and magic have run out and courage is no longer enough? What stories can guide us in the second half of our lives?

Psychotherapist Allan Chinen has made a special study of folk and fairy tales that seek to answer these questions and includes some wonderful examples of "post-heroic" stories in his book *Beyond the Hero*[35]. The most satisfying of these stories follow double cycles in which both the hero's journey and the subsequent post-heroic quest are told. The two cycles have different qualities. The hero's journey takes us out and back, but the post-heroic quest operates on a different plane, taking us down and then back up. It begins not with a call to adventure but by something going wrong that causes us to lose our way. "In the middle of the road of my life I awoke in the *dark wood* where the true way was wholly lost" begins *La Divina Commedia* of Dante Alighieri.

To find the way back, the post-heroic protagonist must stay constant to what he really loves and endure long and difficult labours without the aid of magical interventions. Such are the soulful quests of the second half of life. They take us through the wilderness that lies beyond "happily ever after" to a place of strong, compassionate maturity where we have found our calling, and have learned to be true to what really matters in life rather than obey the dictates of others or the voices of our egos telling us how we ought to behave.

In this chapter, I am going to focus on one particular post-heroic story that I call *The Furthest Shore*. I came across it under another name in the Andrew Lang collection of fairy stories. An illustration of a man fighting a troll fairly leapt off the page at me and as soon as I read the story it intrigued me. It spoke to me of my own life as a man and I was convinced that it would speak to others too. I immediately began to prepare: learning the bare bones of the story, fleshing it out in my imagination, practising with my partner and with friends until I had created a workable version. My first opportunity to tell it to a group of men came in May 2004 at a *Rites of Passage*[36] workshop for men at Cae Mabon in North Wales, to which I had been invited as the guest storyteller. The sheer visceral thrill of the experience is deeply stamped in my memory.

On the Sunday afternoon prior to the workshop, I drove up to Cae Mabon, an encampment in the foothills of Mount Snowdon. There in the fading light I outlined the plot of the story to Ron, the group leader.

"The hero, a fisherman's son brought up by a king, finds his way by magic to a land called The Furthest Shore where he meets his destiny in the form of three princesses imprisoned under a spell. He slays the monsters that have enchanted them and wins the hand of the youngest princess."

I paused and looked at Ron. He looked back, unimpressed. He had heard this kind of story a hundred times. But I had been teasing him. Now for what made this story so different.

"And then, just when you think the story is going to say, 'and they all lived happily ever after', his pride causes him to fall from grace. To redeem himself and to find his way back to The Furthest Shore, he must go out into the world to make a deeper connection with the creatures of the earth, air and sea. He must come to know his life's purpose and make sure that his head, heart and feet are all pointing in the same direction before the North Wind can carry him home to stand alongside his queen as the true king of his own realm."

"That sounds great," Ron said. "Can you do it in three parts, say Monday, Tuesday and wrap it up Thursday evening before our last meal?" I happily agreed and decided to tell it by firelight in the stone roundhouse, the centrepiece of Cae Mabon.

The men coming on the workshop arrived the following day and after we had introduced ourselves and eaten supper, I led them into the darkness of the roundhouse, the only light coming from burning logs in the fire-pit. We sat on the ground and I waited a little as the men settled into silence. Looking round, I could see shadowy outlines and the glint of reflected flames in a dozen pairs of eyes. Leaning forward into the firelight, I began:

Once there was a fisherman who lived with his wife, close to the sea, in a small stone cottage with a thatched roof and front door and window frames made of driftwood. Like his father and grandfather before him, he caught fish for the king's table and delivered them to the palace in the nearby town. He was diligent and skilled and had never failed in his duty.

One day, a day like any other, he pushed his boat down the shingle beach and into the water. He stepped the mast and raised the sail and soon reached his regular fishing grounds. Dropping the sail, he cast his nets and waited… and waited…and waited. The sun rose high in the sky but no fish came. It dropped towards the western horizon but still no fish came. This was unusual but not unknown. The sea was calm and he decided to stay out overnight. By moonlight, he cast his nets and lines but still no fish came.

The next morning, with no wind to drive him, he unshipped the oars and rowed out to deeper waters. He fished the whole of the second day but still no sign of a fish. By now he was getting worried. This had not happened to him before. He stayed out a second night: no fish. By noon of the third day he was getting desperate. Surely he could not fail. How could he return home with no fish for the king's table or his own?

I could sense that the men had begun to relax into the story. Their breathing was steady. They sat still and attentive. I felt a shiver of excitement at being in such a primeval setting: men sitting round a fire in an ancient dwelling in the wilderness, smoke curling up through the thatched roof into the night sky, sharing a timeless tale. Certain now that it would carry us all over the next few days, I went on with the story.

The telling was long, as befits the story of a man's journey through life. That first night took well over half an hour and the other two parts of the story were just as long. I recall how the men groaned involuntarily when the fisherman did a "deal with the devil" in return for a good catch of fish; how they cheered when the hero slew the final troll; how they gleefully offered the names of birds, beasts and fish when asked; how their eyes shone with delight when the hero eventually found his way back to the furthest shore. I remember too my own deep sense of satisfaction at sharing the story for the first time with a group of men.

Since then I have told *The Furthest Shore* many times to other groups, including at a weekend workshop for men, which I ran with Ashley Ramsden at Gaunts House, a joyful and profound experience. Eighteen men shared their lives and met each other through the medium of story. Over the years, the story (which is told in full after this chapter) has become both a mirror in which I can see my own life reflected and a map showing me the way home to my own furthest shore, to the place where I am fully myself.

A few years ago, I spent several weeks in Andalucía, my favourite part of Spain, telling stories and teaching storytelling. Immersed as I was in stories, I decided to spend some of the time writing the story of *The Furthest Shore* as it had developed over the time I had been telling it. There, sitting in a shaded garden, writing on a borrowed laptop, I relived each stage of the protagonist's journey, pausing frequently to reflect on how this story intersected with my own stories and what I could learn from it about my life as a man.

The story begins with the fisherman doing a "deal with the devil" in order to serve the king and to put food on his own table. I remembered, as I wrote, how this passage had prompted so many strong reactions from the men to whom I had told it. At Gaunts House, many had spoken about the duties and responsibilities they were carrying for others - spouses, children, ex-spouses, stepchildren, parents - and the need to stick at unsatisfying and unrewarding work just to get by. Some had felt shame about their failure to develop a career or at being made redundant. Many of the men who had achieved material success resented the price they had paid for it: workaholism and long hours; long-term stress and illness (often hidden from employers); the breakdown of family life and divorce; disconnection from the environmental and social consequences of their work.

What price had I paid for success in the career I had fallen into, I wondered? As a young police officer I was often asked how I managed to deal with sudden death and violence at work and still be a loving husband and father when I got home: "Doesn't it affect you?" And I would reply with what now seemed like wilful self-deception. "Oh no. I have a kind of switch inside that I turn off when I go to work and back on when I get home."

But the trouble was that by the time I reached thirty I had forgotten how to turn the switch back on, and by thirty-five I felt completely hollow and out of touch with my feelings. The price of my career success was, for many years, a narrowing of my horizons and a loss of sensitivity and compassion which, in turn, resulted in increasing alienation from my self and from my wife and children. If only I had been able to see then what I was doing, things might have worked out differently, I thought. Ruefully, I turned back to the keyboard and carried on writing.

The story then moves to a loss of connection between the fisherman and his son who goes to live in the king's court. The difference between the courtly life he experiences and the knowledge of his humble origins is difficult and confusing. I recalled that, when hearing me tell this part of the story, some men had identified strongly with the humble origins of the fisherman's son and had told stories of family hardship, sometimes with pride and sometimes a rankling sense of injustice. Others had spoken of having had more privileged childhoods, although often with painful memories of boarding schools and distant parents.

Their mention of boarding school triggered a memory of

myself as a lost and lonely child, whose father had died when he was four years old and who had been sent to a private school (as the son of working class parents, fees paid by the Royal Air Force Benevolent Fund) with classmates whose parents were doctors, lawyers, academics and diplomats. Consequently, like the fisherman's son, I did not really fit in either at school or at home. I too had been a "fish out of water".

Also like the fisherman's son, I lost a secure sense of connection with my family as I saw how others lived (and, in my case, as I became more academically oriented). Yet at the same time, I was always uncomfortable in the company of boys whose fathers had studies full of books, whose mothers made toast with brown wholemeal bread and honey, and who went skiing and took foreign holidays. I completely understood the desire of the young man in the story who needs to prove himself and wants to be special. His taking to sea alone in his father's boat and surviving the perilous night's journey to find the furthest shore made perfect sense to me.

Lots of young men don't survive the call to adventure. My father died at the age of twenty eight in a plane crash, the consequence of living adventurously. As a young police officer I had seen too many men of my own age die from seeking the thrill of excess speed, overdosing on drugs and alcohol, even committing suicide. Later, two of my closest friends in the police service died in their forties, John of a heart attack and Mick of cancer. But I found myself asking, as I had asked myself many times before, "How come I survived?"

Often, I now reflected, when I am particularly conscious of the life energy in my own body - when I am swimming in the sea or walking in the mountains or sometimes making love - I feel a kind of responsibility to my father and those dead friends, as if their deaths charge me to make the most of my life. I feel more willing to embrace the opportunities for adventure that come my way and much less willing to settle for a life lived anything less than well. With those thoughts echoing in my mind, the story I was writing tugged at my sleeve and demanded that I pick up the threads once more.

The fisherman's son is met on his arrival at *The Furthest*

Shore by an old man who directs him along the strand to meet his destiny. He encounters three princesses and falls in love with the third of them the moment he sees her face. Some of the stories men had shared with me about falling in love and the madness, joy and sheer bloody inconvenience it had brought them had made me laugh - and wince in recognition. "I walked into a room and it was like being hit by a steamroller," one man had told me. "The first time I saw her I thought I had known her all my life," said another. "I was already married, with kids," said a third, "but it didn't make any difference."

It felt painful for me to recall how, as a young man, I had been in too much of a hurry to wait. The third princess did not appear in my life until much later, by which time I was already married with four children. I had known what it was to fall in love instantly and irrevocably. And like the hero of the story, I had learned that the price of love is to allow oneself to be beaten by trolls. Only through acceptance of loss can love flourish. I could see that to live my life fully, I had to allow myself to feel the pain of my father's early death, to grieve my lost lover and let her go, and to embrace the daily agony that comes with seeing my youngest son struggle courageously with a serious physical disability.

In the story, however, that is not the end of the matter. Having defeated the trolls, the young man claims his bride and his share of the kingdom. But then, just when it seems that they will live happily ever, as king and queen of *The Furthest Shore*, it all goes dreadfully wrong. Through foolishness and pride, he loses his queen and his naïve innocence and becomes a wanderer through the wilderness of mid-life. This time he discovers that he is going to need more than courage, luck and a bit of magic to find his way home. I could imagine him asking "How on earth did this happen? How did I end up here?"

In response to the story, men at various workshops had spoken about finding themselves in a kind of wasteland through the vicissitudes of divorce, redundancy, loss of direction, ageing, illness and bereavement. They had spoken too about the struggle that followed and about the opportunities it had brought them for eventually finding new purpose and meaning in their lives. On one thing they had all been agreed: there was no short cut and no easy route back to the furthest shore.

I too empathised with the long hard journey that the wanderer in the story must now make. Like Odysseus adrift on the sea of life, longing for his beloved Ithaka, I was still longing for home, to find my place in the world now that I was freed from the bonds of marriage and career. I thought about spending my life with someone, about creating the work that was truly mine to do, and about what it would mean to live authentically as myself - and not as I imagined others might wish me to. Sitting in that Spanish garden, I picked up my pen and wrote:

> *Somewhere*
> *on this troubled sea*
>
> *there is an island*
> *calling me home.*
>
> *I will find her;*
> *this one whose longing*
>
> *touches my soul,*
> *this one whose fate*
>
> *it is my fate to share,*
> *this one to whom*
>
> *I will say "Yes"*
> *for the rest of my life.*

Finding myself moved by the story, I had instinctively turned to the intense word-images and heightened language of poetry to express myself. In similar circumstances, others might have drawn or painted, sculpted, danced or sung. Responding in these kinds of creative ways to the stories that speak to us helps them continue to act upon us in healing ways. The process is subtle and profound - not a simple cause and effect but an unconscious movement of the soul towards greater wholeness. Often, we cannot see the change happening but looking back later we say to ourselves "Ah, yes. That is where the change began."

The Furthest Shore is a rich and fabulous tale of a man eventually finding his way back home after years of struggle. It provides fresh hope for anyone who has ever lost their way and it has proven to be a wonderful vehicle for men to explore their own journeys through life. My experience of storytelling with men is that the benefits go far beyond individual understanding and healing. Immersing ourselves deeply in a such a shared story can help to create a much-needed sense of male comradeship and community. When men stand together in the face of archetypal masculine stories, when we share our personal stories of love and loss and longing, then we catch a glimpse of something that all men long for.

Although little understood in our culture, there is a particular kind of nurturing that only men can provide for each other. Our tragedy (and the cause of much disappointment in relationships between men and women) is that all too often we men blame our partners for the lack of something we desperately crave and is not theirs to give.

Brotherhood.

The Furthest Shore

Once there was a fisherman who lived with his wife, close to the sea, in a small stone cottage with a thatched roof and front door and window frames made of driftwood. Like his father and grandfather before him, he caught fish for the king's table and delivered them to the palace in the nearby town. He was diligent and skilled and had never failed in his duty.

One day, a day like any other, he pushed his boat down the shingle beach and into the water. He stepped the mast and raised the sail and soon reached his regular fishing grounds. Dropping the sail, he cast his nets and waited... and waited...and waited. The sun rose high in the sky but no fish came. It dropped towards the western horizon but still no fish came. This was unusual but not unknown. The sea was calm and he decided to stay out overnight. By moonlight, he cast his nets and lines but still no fish came.

The next morning, with no wind to drive him, he unshipped the oars and rowed out to deeper waters. He fished the whole of the second day but still no sign of a fish. By now he was getting worried; this had not happened to him before. He stayed out a second night: no fish. By noon of the third day he was getting desperate. Surely he could not fail. How could he return home with no fish for the king's table or his own?

The sun was high overhead, beating down on the flat sea. There was no sign of life, no fish rising to the surface, not a bird in the sky, not a breath of wind. Then suddenly, just a few feet away from the boat, the waters parted and a huge head rose above the surface. It was neither man nor fish, but something of both with long matted sea-weedy hair, large round wet eyes and thick rubbery lips. The creature spoke in a low rumbling voice.

"What is wrong, fisherman?"

"I have been fishing for three days and caught nothing. I cannot stay out at sea any longer but nor can I go home without a catch."

"I can help you. And I want very little in return."

"Tell me, what do you want?"

128

"I will fill your nets with fish. Just bring me whatever your wife first shows to you when you get back home."

And the fisherman, thinking that his wife might greet him with some bread or cakes that she had baked, agreed. The head disappeared below the water.

Soon there was a tug on his lines and he hauled the nets aboard, bulging and heaving with fish. He piled them flapping and gasping on the deck: cod, ling, mackerel, hake, halibut, plaice - a profusion of slippery, gleaming fish. He felt the wind stir, raised the sail and steered his boat homewards. Arriving as dusk fell, he pulled the boat up over the shingles, unloaded his catch and made his way back to the cottage.

He opened the door to greet his wife, full of excitement about his wonderful haul. Before he could speak she held out a small bundle in front of him. "Your baby son," she said. The fisherman suddenly remembered his bargain with the sea creature. "What have I done?" He wept bitter tears as he told his wife about his strange adventure and the promise he had made.

They lay awake long into the night wondering what to do until his wife exclaimed "The Sea shall not have him. We will ask the king to look after him. Surely he will be safe in the palace away from here!" Next day, the fisherman went to the palace and asked for an audience with the king. The king was not an unkind man and when he heard of the fisherman's plight, he agreed to take his son into the palace. "We will bring him up as one of our own children."

So the fisherman's son grew up alongside the young princes and princesses in the palace. He was well treated, given the very best hand-me-down clothes and taught how a gentleman should behave. The years passed. Occasionally he caught a glimpse of his father when he came to the palace to deliver fish and one day, when he had grown into a fine young man, he asked leave of the king to spend a day with his real father and mother.

They were delighted to see him and when he asked his father to show him how to catch fish he agreed to take him out in his boat. After all, many years had passed, his son was no longer a child, what harm could come to them now? Father and son spent the day out on the water, catching fish with nets and lines and when the *day was done returned safely to the shore.*

Together they unstepped the mast and hauled the boat onto the shingle beach. As the fisherman finished unloading the fish, lines and nets the young man looked about himself and patted the pockets in his jacket and breeches. "I have lost my handkerchief," he said. "It must have gone over the side. I'm sure I can find it." Before his father could stop him he had shoved the boat back down into the water, jumped in and rowed out into the foaming waves. His father ran to the water's edge. "Stop, stop. Come back." But it was too late, by this time the boat was out beyond the breakers and travelling swiftly out to sea. He watched the boat carry his son into the gloom of the falling dusk until it was out of sight.

The young man quickly realised that he was in trouble. The waves got up and rocked the boat so violently that he could no longer row. Dusk gave way to a moonless night. Clouds covered the stars and the sea drove the boat onwards and onwards through the inky blackness so that all he could do was to hang on to the sides and hope that he would somehow survive the onslaught.

Who knows if it was one night or many that the young man spent at sea? The darkness and the rushing sea seemed to go on forever. Eventually, long after he had given up hope of ever returning home, the sky began to lighten and the sea to calm. Dawn came and the sea carried him steadily on towards the rising sun. In the distance he noticed a white line stretching as far as he could see across the horizon. As he got closer, he could see that it was a beach: a long, low strand of white sand. The boat bumped gently ashore and he jumped out and kissed the ground in gratitude and relief for surviving his journey.

He stood up and looked around. The sea lapped gently on the shore. It was unnaturally silent with no sign of birds or other life. Inland, rocky outcrops and tall sand dunes ranged as far as the eye could see. Suddenly one of the rocks nearby seemed to move and when the young man looked more closely he could see that it was the figure of an old man, dressed in a robe of brown sackcloth with white flowing hair and beard, his skin like old parchment and eyes as blue as the sea itself.

The figure reached out a bony hand and beckoned him. "Who are you and where do you come from?" asked the old man. So the fisherman's son told him about his parents, how he had been brought up in a palace, and how the sea had carried him to this place through the night. "But I don't know where I am sir, or indeed who you are."

"You have told your story well, young man. I am called the Watcher and you have arrived at the Furthest Shore. I can tell you that your destiny is waiting for you here if you wish to meet it." The young man's heart leapt with excitement. "There is nothing I want more. Please tell me what I must do."

"Go north along the strand and you will eventually come to a strange sight. Three sisters, princesses, are buried in the sand with only their heads visible. They are held there as prisoners, under a spell. They will entreat you to release them. The first to speak will be the eldest, do not listen to her but go on. The second to speak will be the middle sister, ignore her pleas and go on. The third will be the youngest sister. Listen to her and she will tell you what is needed to break the enchantment."

The young man thanked the Watcher and made his way north along the strand trudging all day through the heat of the sun as it rose high overhead and the cool of the afternoon as it dropped low in the sky. Just before dusk he saw ahead of him three shapes protruding from the sand. He went up to the first. It was a woman's head, looking out to sea, encrusted with salt and quite motionless like a statue. As he reached out and touched it, the salt crust cracked open and fell away.

"Save me, save me," said the disembodied head. "Save me and you shall marry me and half the realm will be yours." Her cries were pitiful and her face beautiful but he remembered the Watcher's instructions and went to the second shape... seemingly identical to the first. Again, the salt mask fell away as he touched it.

"Save me, save me," said the second head. "Save me and you shall marry me and half the realm will be yours." He ignored her pleas and went on to the third shape and once again revealed the face trapped beneath the salt shell.

"Save us, save us," said the third. "Save us all three if you can and you shall choose among us if you wish and share this realm with whomsoever you marry." The youngest princess was as beautiful as she was generous and fair-minded. Her long dark hair, released from its cake of salt, blew in the breeze, her bright green eyes sparkled in the evening light and her lips parted in a warm smile. This time he stopped to listen.

"I will save you if I can. Tell me what I must do."

"Our land and our castle have been taken from us by trolls who keep us trapped here under a spell. If you would release us and free the land, you must go inland tonight until you find the road which leads to the gate of our castle. Two fierce lions guard the gate. You must show no fear but walk between them, your head held high, into the courtyard. Then look for a room in the deepest, darkest recess of the castle. There is a bed in it and you must lie down and wait. In the small hours of the night a troll will come into the room and beat you with staves. You must let the troll beat you and only when he has finished may you reach for the bottle of salve and the sword that hangs on the wall behind the bed. Use the salve to heal your wounds and the sword to slay the troll."

The young man heard the princess's words and thought them the sweetest he had ever heard, for he had fallen in love with her the first moment he saw her face. "I will do it," he said.

"Are you sure?" said the princess. "It is a dreadful thing to ask."

"I will do it for you," said the young man.

Straight away he said farewell to the princess and made his way inland through the gathering gloom until he found his feet upon a broad highway. Soon the shadowed shape of the castle appeared before him and he went towards the gate. Two lions roared and snarled at him as he approached but he held his head high and showed no fear as he passed between them, their hot breath on his neck. Inside the courtyard there was no sign of life, no servants, horses, carriages, no voices, music or clattering of dishes, just an eerie silence. In the deepest, darkest corner of the castle he found a room with a hard iron bedstead and, hanging on the wall behind, a small glass bottle and a bright sword. He lay down on the bed and waited.

In the small hours of the night he heard the sound of drunken voices singing and yelling far off in the castle then the tread of heavy footsteps approaching his room. Heart pounding, he gritted his teeth and squinted through half-closed eyes as the door was flung open and, silhouetted by lantern light, he saw the giant scaly figure of a troll with three heads and three arms. "What is this? They dare send a boy to free them. We'll soon see about that!" roared the troll. From his belt he took three wooden staves and thrashed the young man as he lay on the bed until all three staves were broken. As the troll turned to leave, the young man took down the bottle and poured the salve on his wounds. The strength came back into his body and he took the sword in his hands. With three swift cuts he slashed off each of the troll's three heads and the troll crashed dead to the floor like an ox that had been poleaxed. Replacing the sword and the salve, the young man stepped over the corpse and swiftly made his way out of the castle and back to the shore.

It was dawn when he arrived and by the early morning light, he could see that the three princesses had been released from the sand, but only as far as their waists. He went over to the youngest princess and knelt to greet her. She thanked and embraced him, tears of love and gratitude running down her face. He smiled back at her. "I can see that my work is not yet done."

"No, my dear, I fear you must return to the castle tonight. You will meet a second troll, more terrible than the first. If you would free us then you must do as you did before. It is a dreadful thing to ask."

"I will do it for you," said the young man, kissing her hand.

They spent the day together, talking of this and that, as young lovers do. When night fell the young man made his way back to the castle, passing between the two lions and into the room where he had spent the previous night. The slain troll had vanished and he lay down on the lonely bed and waited. Once more, in the small hours, he heard the sound of drunken voices and heavy footsteps approaching. This time, when the door flew open he saw a troll with six heads and six arms, each hand holding a wooden stave. With a guttural roar, the troll launched himself at the bed, raining blows on the young man until each of the six staves was broken. The pain was terrible, there were purple bruises and raised welts all over his body. As the troll turned to leave, he reached for the bottle and poured the healing salve on his wounds and as the strength came back into his body he took the sword in his hands.

With six swingeing cuts he slashed off each of the troll's six heads and the troll crashed dead to the floor like a doomed oak in the forest. Replacing the sword and the salve once more, the young man stepped over the corpse and returned to his sweetheart by the shore.

The three princesses had been released from the sand, but only as far as their knees. He went over to the youngest princess who was overjoyed to see him. "You have done your work bravely and well, but all is not yet done. I fear you must return to the castle tonight. You will meet a third troll, even more terrible than the others. If you would free us then you must do as you did before. Third time pays all."

"I will do it for you," said the young man.

That night he returned once more to that dreadful chamber. The corpse of the second troll, like that of the first, had vanished and he lay down on the bed to wait for the coming of the third troll. In the small hours of the night, when the human spirit is at its lowest ebb and the wisdom and courage of the daylight are far away, the door was flung open to reveal the monstrous figure of a troll with nine heads and nine arms, a wooden stave in each hand. The troll spat at the figure on the bed. "Neither you, nor your magic are any match for me, you upstart whelp." With that he delivered a furious volley of blows and this time the young man could not keep quiet. He screamed and sobbed as the staves crashed into him. His flesh burst open like an over-ripe plum, blood poured from his wounds and he heard the sound of his own ribs cracking as he passed out in a dead faint.

The troll continued his beating on and on until the last stave was broken, then he picked up the limp body and threw it contemptuously against the wall before turning to leave the room. But the young man's body had struck the very place where the salve and the sword were hanging. The glass bottle shattered and the healing liquid poured itself over his wounds bringing life and strength back into his limbs. He grasped the bright sword in both hands and flew at the troll like a demon hacking and slashing at his heads until he had severed all nine and the dead troll crumpled to the ground like an avalanche tumbling down a mountain.

The young man ran back to the beach and when he arrived

he saw that the three princesses had been released from the sand. They were laughing and dancing together in the shallow water. The youngest princess ran over to him, threw her arms around his neck and kissed his face. "You have saved us all and now, if you wish, you shall choose which of us to marry." And the young man said "Can you doubt that it is you with whom I wish to share this realm and you I wish to marry?" She willingly accepted his proposal and they went back to the castle to get married.

Time passed and life returned to the realm. Those who had been in hiding came back out into the light. Crops were planted, flocks tended and the land prospered. The two elder sisters went off to other lands with husbands of their own and the young king and his queen lived happily together for many years. That is, until the trouble really began.

One day, the young king turned to his queen and said, "I have been thinking about my mother and father. The last they knew of me I was heading out to sea. They certainly don't know that I have become a king. Why, they probably think I am dead. I would so like to go back and see them."

"I don't think that would be wise, my dear," said the queen. "Surely your place is here with me."

But the young king would not let the matter drop and eventually the queen said "Very well, if you must go then go you must. But I give you this warning: pay heed to what your father says and not to what your mother asks of you. I can help you make this journey." She slipped a silver ring off her finger and onto his. "This ring has magic in it. It will grant you two wishes… to wish yourself back to your parents' house and then to return safely home to me."

No sooner had the young king wished himself back to his parents' house than he was standing outside the door to their cottage. He knocked and when the door was opened there stood his father and behind him, sitting by the fire, his mother. At first they did not recognise him in his fine robes. "Father, mother," he said. "It's me, your son." When they could see who he really was, they wept. "We thought you were dead." Then the tears turned to laughter and they hugged each other and all talked at once. "Why, look at you in your fine clothes. Wherever have you been?" said his mother.

Over the next few days they told each other about the lives they had led since they were last together. The fisherman and his wife had carried on much the same, although deeply grieved by losing their only son to the sea, as they thought, and they were astonished to learn that he had not only survived but had married a princess and become king in a distant land. "You should go to the palace," said his mother. "You'd show that old king a thing or two. Look at you. I'm so proud of you."

His father counselled against it. "I fear we'll have no more joy of you in this lifetime if you go to the palace. Enough is enough. Let us simply enjoy being together until it is time for you to return to your queen."

But it was his mother's words to which he listened. His wife's warning slipped from his mind. He wanted to go to the palace. He wanted to show the old king a thing or two, to show him that - fisherman's son or not - he was as good a king as he.

So he did visit the palace where he had been brought up and he stood before the throne, not in the very best hand-me-downs, but in robes finer than those worn by the old king himself. He was graciously received and the two kings talked of royal matters: of the loyalty and warmth of their subjects; of the opulence of their treasuries; of the extent and prosperity of their lands. And on each point the young king bested his elder. Exasperated, the old king said "Your subjects may be more numerous, your treasuries richer and your lands more extensive but I'll warrant your queen is not as fair as mine."

"My queen is the wisest, most beautiful and virtuous woman to be found in any realm," boasted the young king. "I wish she was here before us now so that you could see for yourself."

At that moment, a strange hush fell over them; the old king and his courtiers froze as if they were wax dummies in a tableau, the curtains covering the doorway swept aside and the young king's bride stepped into the room. Looking only at him, she spoke quietly. "What have you done? The ring had only two wishes in it and now you have used them both. I cannot live here and how will you ever find your way back to the Furthest Shore without its power?"

Tears welled up in the young king's eyes as he realised his terrible mistake. His queen went over to him and slipped the ring off his finger. Then she kissed his cheek and smoothed his head with her hand. "Remember me," she said and tenderly plaited the ring into his hair. "Farewell, dearest man." Then she turned on her heel and walked out the room, curtains swishing closed behind her.

Instantly the figures in the room unfroze. "What was that? Who was she?" the old king asked. He got no answer because the young king had dashed through the curtains calling after his queen. "Come back, come back. I'm sorry, I'm sorry." It was too late, she had disappeared and no one, not even the palace guards had seen her come and go. They searched the palace and the palace grounds; soldiers were sent out to scour the countryside but she was nowhere to be found.

Desolate, the young king determined that somehow, no matter how hard and long the quest, he would find his way back to the Furthest Shore, he would be reunited with the bride he loved. He left the old king's palace, said goodbye to his parents and exchanged his fine robes for hard-wearing breeches and traveller's cloak. Not knowing where to go, he roamed the land aimlessly asking everyone he came across if they knew the way to the Furthest Shore but always he was met with a puzzled look and a shake of the head.

On and on he went, sleeping under hedges, in barns and outhouses, sometimes sharing food with farmers or the warmth of a campfire with hunters in return for his labour or the telling of his tale. The weeks turned into months and the months into years. His long hair and his beard streaked with grey, his face weather-beaten by the trail, his body lean and hardened by hardship and sorrow, he never gave up. He wandered far from the old king's realm into lands unmapped and untracked, hoping always for some hint or clue of the way home.

One day, he found himself at a clearing deep in the heart of an ancient forest. Before him stood a bear of a man nearly twice his height, dressed in furs, his hand stroking the shoulder of a stag. "I don't know who you are sir but I'm guessing this is your forest. Pardon my trespass, I am searching for the way back to the Furthest Shore. Can you help me please?"

The man replied in a deep rumbling voice. "You are welcome here. I am the lord of the beasts of the earth. I do not know the way back to the Furthest Shore but perhaps my creatures can help." He pulled a great ox horn from under his fur cloak and blew a sonorous blast that echoed into the trees. All kinds of beasts appeared: wolves, badgers, porcupines, lions, deer, squirrels, boars, monkeys, snakes. All the beasts that run, walk, crawl or slither on the ground gathered around them. "Do any of you know the way back to the Furthest Shore?" he asked. But none of the creatures knew the way.

"I am sorry we cannot help you. Perhaps my brother will know; he is the lord of the birds and the beasts of the air. Put these on," he said, handing the traveller a pair of fur lined boots. "Follow where your feet lead and you will find him. When you do find him, give him my regards - and remember to send the boots back."

So the traveller set off, letting the boots lead him, walking for many days and miles until he came to the bare summit of a mountain. Before him stood a tall, slender man with sharp aquiline features wearing a cape, a hawk perched on his wrist. "I'm guessing that you are the lord of the birds and the beasts of the air and that this is your domain. Pardon my trespass; I bring greetings from your brother, the lord of the beasts of the earth. He lent me these boots to find you. I am looking for the way back to the Furthest Shore. Can you help me please?"

The man spoke in a high lilting tone. "Take the boots off, they will return to my brother of their own accord." The traveller did so. "You are welcome here. I do not know the way back to the Furthest Shore but perhaps my creatures will know." From under his feathered cloak he took a pipe made from the wing bone of an albatross and blew a shrill note that echoed around the mountaintop. Soon, all manner of birds and flying creatures appeared: blackbirds, doves, eagles, bats, dragonflies, crows, humming birds, gulls, plovers and pigeons. All the birds and creatures that fly, buzz and flap in the air circled around their heads. "Do any of you know the way back to the Furthest Shore?" he asked. But none of them knew the way.

"I am sorry we cannot help you. Perhaps my brother will know; he is the lord of the fish and the creatures of the deep. Put these on," he said, handing the traveller a pair of soft downy boots. "Follow where your feet lead and you will find him. Give him my regards -

and remember to send the boots back."

So the traveller set off once again, letting the boots lead him, walking for many days and miles until he came to the top of a cliff. Before him, looking out to sea, stood a lithe and willowy man with damp hair and a cloak of sharkskin. A young seal played about his feet. "I'm guessing that you are the lord of the fish and the creatures of the deep and that this is your domain," said the traveller. "Pardon my trespass; I bring greetings from your brother, the lord of the birds and beasts of the air. He lent me these boots to find you. I am looking for the way back to the Furthest Shore. Can you help me please?"

The man spoke in soft, liquid tones. "Take the boots off, they will return to my brother of their own accord." The traveller did so. "You are welcome here. I do not know the way back to the Furthest Shore but perhaps one of my creatures will know. Follow me." He led the way down a steep path to the sea. There he waded out until the water lapped round his waist. From under his cloak he took a long whalebone paddle and slapped the surface of the water sending shock waves through the ocean currents. Soon all manner of fish and creatures of the deep appeared: marlin, tuna, swordfish, octopus, crabs, whales, porpoises, shrimps and seahorses, all the fish and creatures of the deep swimming around them.

"Do any of you know the way back to the Furthest Shore?" he asked. But all were silent until up spoke an old pike. "Yes, I know the way. Indeed I am shortly on my way there. You see, in my human form I am a cook at the castle there and I must help to prepare a feast. They say the queen is to be married again. She has been alone these many years and now another man has come to take her husband's place."

Married again? Surely not; to be so close after so many years of searching only to lose her at the last. The traveller could not bear the thought. "Can you take me there?"

"I am sorry," said the pike. "It is not possible. I must swim under the water and you would drown."

"Perhaps there is a way," said the lord of the deeps. "My creatures cannot take you but if you go back up the cliff you will find, not far from here, a heath. On that heath are three brothers: one has a hat, one a cloak and one a pair of boots. They cannot decide which belongs to what or what belongs to whom. They have been fighting over them for many years. It is said that whoever wears the hat, the cloak and the boots together can wish themselves wherever they want to be. If you can persuade these brothers to part with them, perhaps you will be able to return to the Furthest Shore after all."

The traveller thanked the pike and the lord of the deeps and rushed back up the cliff to find the three brothers and soon he spied them on the heath, yelling, shoving and pushing, wrestling each other to the ground, snatching the hat and the cloak and the boots from each other in turn in a mad merry-go-round of mayhem and discord.

"Stop," called out the traveller. "What is this you are doing?"

"We have been fighting for a hundred years," replied one of the brothers. "Ouch... those boots are mine... give me that hat... you are not going to have my cloak." Round and round they went.

"A hundred years," said the traveller. "Aren't you getting tired? I could sort this out for you. Let me try on the hat and the cloak and the boots and I will soon know which belongs to each of you, then you can stop fighting and go about your business."

This seemed like a good idea to the brothers so they called a truce and handed over each item to the traveller to try on. He put on the hat and his mind became crystal clear; he wrapped the cloak around his chest and felt his heart open wide; he pulled on the boots and his will became indomitable. He wished himself back home on the Furthest Shore and as he did so, he rose into the air with the three brothers shaking their fists and cursing at him far below.

The North Wind caught him up in his arms. "I will take you home," said the wind. "And when we get there, I will put you down at the castle gate. Stand aside then and I will rattle and blow and shake the windows and doors so hard that that impostor will come to see what is happening and I will whisk him away."

Flying high in the air above land and sea he soon saw ahead the white strand of the Furthest Shore and the castle where he had suffered so much and known so much joy. True to his word, the North Wind set him down at the gate and he stood to one side as the wind rattled and shook at the windows and doors. The castle gate opened and out stepped a man, not unlike himself, to see what was happening and the North Wind picked him up and whisked him away so that he never came back - in this story at least. The wind died away and the king of the Furthest Shore, in his traveller's clothes once more, entered the courtyard and climbed the stone stairs to the throne room.

He stood by the doorway for a long moment. There she stood, turned half away from him, hand resting on the back of her throne. She turned fully towards him and looked quizzically as if she did not recognise him. She approached him slowly, her long dark hair flowing down her back, her eyes bright green just as he had remembered her each night and each day of his long quest. His breath caught and his heart quickened as he looked at her. He had no words to say and silent tears ran down his cheeks. She looked at his lined face, his grey-streaked hair and beard, and saw the tenderness in his tear-filled eyes. Could this be him? Then something glinted silver in his hair and she reached out and touched the ring she had plaited there so long ago.

"Oh, my dearest man, I hoped and prayed for your return. I waited such a long time for you that I thought you must be dead. You have come back to me and all is well." They fell into each other's arms, hardly believing their good fortune after their long separation.

That evening, the feast that had been prepared was put to good use as they celebrated the true king's return and renewed their marriage vows. After the food and drink came music and dancing, masques and merriment before retiring for the night. And the king and queen of the Furthest Shore lived in love and happiness, ruling wisely and well until the end of their days on earth.

About the story

This story appears as *The Three Princesses of Whiteland* in Andrew Lang's *Red Fairy Book* which was first published in 1890. Lang himself took it from a story collected in the mid 19th Century by Norwegian folklorist Jørgen Moe. The version above is the one that I have developed through telling the story over many years. It stays quite true to the original although some details are my own invention.

12
Fathers & Sons

"It is not flesh and blood but the heart which makes us fathers and sons," wrote Friedrich von Schiller over two hundred years ago. The father-son relationship is one of the most important and problematic relationships for most men. We want our father's love and approval yet we must distance ourselves from him if we are ever to become our own men. In how many fairy stories must the king - that archetypal symbol of the father - be slain in order that the young man can claim his rightful place in the world?

Later in life, coming to terms with one's father (who he really is or was rather than the idealised and demonised images of our youth) becomes an essential developmental task for men. To see our fathers as fallible human beings and still to love them and be grateful for what they have given us provides a secure place from which to accept our own gifts and fallibility as we move into middle age and elderhood.

In this chapter I want to show how, by acting as a bridge between the visible exterior world around us and the invisible interior worlds of memory and imagination, storytelling can help us heal the father-son relationship. Sometimes, if we trust ourselves to follow a story wherever it goes, we cross that bridge to the invisible world and - in memory and imagination - we encounter people and places inaccessible to us in daily life. On rare occasions, on the other side of that bridge, we might even be able to put right something that went wrong long ago.

For most of my life I had no memory of my father. He was an RAF pilot and died in a plane crash during a training mission when I was four years old. To this day, my most prized possession is a grainy black and white photograph of a Lancaster bomber, an air-to-air shot of my father flying somewhere over East Anglia a few months before the accident. If you look closely, it is just possible to make out his figure in the pilot's seat.

Since I had no memory of him, all that I had were photographs and stories: pictures of an impossibly handsome young man in uniform and the idealised stories of those who die before their time. When I was a seven year old child at boarding school, the stories sustained me in my loneliness. They served me well; they helped me survive.

As a young man, I unconsciously sought to emulate him when I joined the police service (another uniformed organisation) and worked my way up the ranks, thinking occasionally that he might have been proud of what I had achieved. I wished that I had known him but still did not realise how big a void his death had left in my life. Increasingly as the years passed and the apparently secure frameworks of marriage, family and career began to totter, I yearned for him.

It was that yearning that took me to various men's workshops in my mid-forties. Talking to other men at one such workshop, I became aware how much I still defined myself in terms of the little boy whose daddy had died and how little sense I had of myself as a person in my own right. When we were invited to tell our own life stories in the form of a fable, I began with an account of his life and death. Remembering the photograph of him flying the Lancaster, I imagined him to be a Dragon Rider with me as *The Dragon Rider's Son*, which is what I called the story. There were nine of us on the workshop at Roeburndale, a remote valley in Lancashire, and we each wrote our stories and read them to each other, sitting by a campfire.

The final line of my written story had been "I am the Dragon Rider's son". But when I read it aloud, some words came completely unbidden and I added: "But what is *my* name?" In that moment I knew that I had to find a way to lay my father's ghost to rest and come to a new relationship with him, in order that I might redefine myself from "the little boy whose father was killed when he was four" to a person in my own right, a product but not a prisoner of my past. The stories that I had carried inside me for so many years, of my father as an unknown dead hero, were no longer enough. I needed some new stories, ones that made him real.

The phrase "But what is *my* name?" unlocked the floodgate. A few weeks later, back at Roeburndale for another workshop, on 18 June 1995, which happened to be Father's Day, I was in for a surprise. Late in the afternoon I went for a solitary walk and lay down to look through the wooden slats of a rickety footbridge suspended over a river. It was bright sunshine, although it had rained heavily the night before, and the sunlight glittered on the swollen blood-red torrent as it rushed beneath me. I was mesmerised by the scintillating light half-blinding my eyes and the sound of the water filling my ears with what sounded like a wild song.

Forgetting that I was supposed to be a sensible grown-up man, I sang back to the river in hoarse, high-pitched tones that were snatched away by the rushing water. This strange and unexpected musical conversation seemed to expand my consciousness. Roeburndale was an ancient, unspoiled valley and I was willing to believe it still had magic. My rational mind relaxed its grip and I felt completely present and wide open to everything around me.

In that moment I noticed a charred tree-stump caught on a rock, swaying in the current. And in some extraordinary fashion that I can neither explain nor describe, though it did not change shape, it became my father's body. My heart pounding, I stumbled into the water and dragged him ashore. I could feel his presence so strongly that I sat on the bank with my arms around the tree-stump and I - the man who had forgotten how to cry - cried like the child I had been when he died. I could imagine that the river was weeping too, his tears perhaps. In that way, we cried together for what we had both lost when he died. We cried and we laughed at the impossible joy of being together again.

"I have missed you so much," I said aloud.

"You are my son. I love you," was his wordless reply.

We stayed together by the river bank until dusk and

then I carried the tree-stump up the steep side of the valley and placed it on a boulder so that he could keep guard over me sleeping down below at the campsite. That night I slept a sweet, dreamless sleep as though resting like a child in his arms without any care or burden.

The next morning I told the other men about my experience and led them up through the long, wet grass to the tree-stump perched on the boulder. As we arrived at the boulder, a solitary fighter jet passed high overhead in the sky above like a sign saying "I am here". I wept again for my father, this time as a man surrounded by other men, feeling the strength of their arms as they held me up, seeing their own tears falling and mingling with mine on the ground - a libation for all our fathers.

My belief was that he had come to me to say goodbye, had come for me to return him to the friendly earth and mourn him as I had been unable to do as a child. It was time to let go of a ghost so that I could have a real father - one who had lived well and died early. As I sat on the boulder beside my father's image, some of the other men dug a grave in a small wild garden by the river. When they returned, we carried the tree-stump in a funeral procession and placed it in the ground. Together, we covered it with soil and smoothed the earth down as if tucking him in bed under a green quilt. Then someone asked if I wanted to say anything. I thought for a moment and the words came easily:

My father could fly - and it cost him his life. He was a strong man, a loving man, and fearless. If he had been different, he might have lived longer, but he died doing what he loved best and I am proud of him. His name was Raymond Geoffrey Mead and he died in 1953, aged twenty-eight years. Thank you for helping me to bury him today. Goodbye Dad - I love you - Rest in Peace.

Looking back on this after many years, during which I have found immense support in the knowledge that my father lived and died, loving me, I realise that without the story of the *Dragon Rider's Son* as a catalyst, it would not have happened.

The question that arose for me at the end of the story made me realise that I had reached a point in my life where I was ripe for change. It was as though the tectonic plates of my subconscious mind were signalling their readiness to shift, like the tremors and shocks that sometimes prefigure an earthquake. Thus, when I heard the river "singing" to me in Roeburndale, that subconscious part of my mind took over and I simply sang back. The supernatural meeting with my father that resulted from that exchange dramatically changed the nature of our relationship. I came to see him as a man of flesh and blood, an ancestor upon whom I could rely as a solid foundation for my own life.

And yet still I regretted that I had no memory of him when he was alive. Until very recently, that is, when I sat up in bed one morning and recalled a conversation I had had with my mother a few weeks before. A story began to form in my mind so I grabbed my laptop and wrote it just as it emerged as a piece of "freefall writing"[37].

I am three and a half years old and I am riding my tricycle. It is almost a toy one, too small for me. My chubby legs are going round and I tug at the handlebars, standing up and moving the bike physically, dragging it round the corners when I cannot steer it. Mum and Dad are walking along the drive, the long drive of the old house, near me. They are laughing and chatting, their words floating over me. I don't pay attention to the words, I just love the sound of their voices close to me. It is an autumn day, late summer maybe, I am warm but not too hot. I have a red cardigan on, buttoned up, and khaki shorts, buckle shoes and grey ankle socks. The bike starts to feel heavy. It is hard work dragging it round, trying to peddle at the front wheel only. I get fed up with it and get off. There is a break in the fence, a five bar gate, solid, wooden and high. I run over to it, reach up and grab a bar above my head and step up onto the bottom rail, then reach up again and bring my left leg higher onto the next rail. I am climbing because I can and because Mum and Dad are there to catch me if I fall.

"Come down, Geoffrey," Mum calls but although I understand what she is saying I don't stop. "Come down. You might fall and hurt yourself," she says. I look round, not wanting to stop but knowing that I must respond somehow to this voice. I glance at Dad. "It is all right," he says. "Let him climb." "But he might fall," says Mum. "Yes, he might. But he won't go far and it is how he has to learn. You cannot climb without the risk of falling. But he will be all right. Let him climb."

It is a complicated conversation, I am not quite sure what has gone on between them but I can sense that I have their permission to carry on. Reach up, grab the bar, step up to the next rail, hand over hand, foot over foot, I get to the top of the gate and turn round triumphant. Dad reaches over, puts his hands under my armpits and lifts me off the gate, high into the air, above his head, whizzing me round and round like an aeroplane, like one of the planes he flies when he is not at home with mummy and me. Then he brings me lower and lower, still whizzing round and round until my feet brush the ground and then he slows down and brings me to a halt on the grass.

"Safe landings," he says. "Happy landings." I get up under my own steam and go back to the trike. "We have to get that boy another bike," says Dad. "That one is getting much too small for him."

That Christmas Mum spent two months' worth of her widow's pension buying me a new bike. A red Triang tricycle with whitewall tyres, a shiny silver bell, proper brakes and pedals that made the back wheels go round not the front one, it had a boot at the back, a lid that opened up to put things in and I loved it. But it wasn't the same; nothing was ever the same again.

Safe landings, happy landings, Dad.

It is the kind of story that takes twenty minutes to write - fifty eight years and twenty minutes. It strikes me as a seminal moment, an iconic story from my life. Is it Mum's story or my story or even Dad's story? You could say that it is my story from Mum's recollection but I'm not sure it matters how we describe it. What really matters is that Mum could smile as she told me and that I could feel my way back into that time and place, could sense the love and support of both my parents and retell the story through the immediacy of my own imagination in a way that brings me joy and comfort. All memories are stories of a kind and now I have a memory of Dad before he died.

As a storyteller, I love the heightened language of traditional stories that conveys so well the connection between the everyday and the archetypal. But in these stories of my relationship with my father, I can also see that plain, vernacular, descriptive language is quite enough to tell a powerful story and that the healing power of storytelling can be experienced without straying into mythic realms. The most important thing, I realise, is simply to tell the story *as a story*, rather than as a history.

13
Sons & Fathers

Sometimes the stories we most need to tell are the most difficult to put into words. This is especially true when the story is of someone close to you like a father or a son. During a recent workshop on autobiographical storytelling I eventually decided, after much heart-searching, to tell the story of my son Tom's life as a man living with a severe physical disability. It was enormously challenging to let go of technique and simply "tell it from the heart". I learned that my task - as storyteller and as father - was to share, in a spirit of humility and generosity, the inspiring gifts that my son's courage and magnanimity have brought into my life.

At first, I had no inkling that it would be Tom's story that I would eventually choose to tell. "What we are going to do this week," said Roi, the teacher, to the group on the first evening of the workshop, "is to find special moments from our own lives and offer them as gifts to each other. We'll work together to find what is archetypal and universal in them so that you can give something meaningful to your listeners. Then we'll craft these experiences so that you each have an autobiographical story to share with the group at the end of the week."

This would be easy, I thought. I knew how to craft a story. I was familiar with the seductive power of words, the neat turn of phrase, the rhythms and repetitions that are the storyteller's stock in trade. Then too, my ego told me, I had lived a varied and interesting life - surely making a story from some titbit of experience would not be too difficult. But over the next few days, I was to discover just how wrong I was.

The first problem I encountered turned out to be choosing

what experience to base the story on. Each time we did an exercise I tried something different: the perils of falling in love with the wrong person; a dramatic incident from my police career; a tricky moment sailing in the Aegean; the adventure of driving my beloved Morgan sports car across Spain with my partner.

Technically, I could do the exercises - creating an arresting opening, developing characters, describing moments of tension - quite easily. It was just that nothing had any real passion or conviction for me in the telling. And while the other course members seemed to settle quite quickly on the stories they were going to tell at the end of the week, I continued to flit from one story to another for several days, more focused on the craft than the content of what I told. Each evening in my room, I wondered why I was finding it so difficult to choose a subject for my story. It was as though my story-engine was racing but the clutch was slipping and I could not connect its power to the road-wheels. I became increasingly unsettled and anxious that I would make a fool of myself in front of my fellow storytellers.

I knew that I was missing something important but I just could not put my finger on it until, on the penultimate day of the course, I asked Roi what I should do. He smiled and replied "It is the simplest and sometimes the most difficult thing in the world: just speak from the heart." His words sank into me like pebbles dropped lightly into a pond slowly finding their way to the bottom. I ruminated on them all afternoon as I sat in a semi-circle of other course members, listening to several of them tell their tales. Some stories were told with skill and sophistication whilst others were related without any guile or ornament. It was clear that all of the experiences on which they were based were highly significant for the tellers and some of them touched me deeply.

Paolo, for example, told us the story of an old man he had met who lived very simply in a shed in the compound of a glove factory he had once owned. When the man had reached the age of seventy, he had given the factory away to the workers. "Just to be in his presence was to feel the glow of his goodness and generosity," said Paolo. "He did not seem to want or need anything. Meeting him inspired me to change my life. I left my job and now I work in a Camphill community caring for people with learning disabilities."

Later, Eleanor - now past retirement age and walking with the aid of a stick - told us how, when she had been a very young girl in India, her mother had woken her in the middle of the night for a surprise: "Something you will remember for the rest of your life". Bundled up in blankets against the cold, the family had driven for hours up a mountain road in the Himalayan foothills and waited until dawn to watch the sun rise, flooding its pink and gold light over Everest and the surrounding valleys. "My mother was right," concluded Eleanor. "That image has stayed with me every day of my life as fresh and bright as when I first saw it. Even in difficult times it has brought me hope."

Gradually, as their stories unfolded, I realised that the tellers were not trying to be clever, not attempting to instruct us or to make a particular point. Paolo and Eleanor were simply sharing, in a heartfelt way, gifts that others had brought into their lives; their stories were so touching because they themselves had been deeply touched by the people and events they described. As we ended the session that afternoon and I went back to my room pondering the stories I had heard, it occurred to me that in storytelling as in life, perhaps the greatest gifts we have to give are ones that others have given us. With that thought, I finally knew what story I had to tell when it came to my turn the next morning. I also knew that this would be one occasion when my skill and experience as a storyteller would count for little. I would have to find other resources than skill to do justice to what I wanted to tell and deeper reserves than storytelling experience to sustain me in the telling.

Despite these anxieties, having found my story, I slept well that night and woke up the next day with a sense of anticipation. After breakfast, we gathered once more in our now familiar semi-circle and when Roi invited the next person to come forward, I stood up and made my way to the storyteller's chair.

I looked around at the smiling faces of the small audience, pausing to catch their eyes and make a personal connection with each one of them by silently recalling moments from the stories they had already told. Then I was ready to begin.

After listening to all your stories yesterday, I realised that what I really want to do is tell you something about my son Tom. I don't even know if what I have to say is a story as such: more of a praise song, perhaps, to someone who is my hero and greatest teacher.

Tom is twenty-five years old and he has a condition called Friedreich's Ataxia that restricts him to a wheelchair and makes all forms of mobility very difficult. The symptoms - loss of balance and control over his limbs - came on when he was about thirteen and it took another couple of years to get a proper diagnosis so he has been wrestling with this for over a decade now.

How did this happen? Well, there is a genetic story. Friedreich's Ataxia is what they call "recessive". It turns out that Tom's mother and I both unknowingly carried a particular rare gene in our DNA that created a one-in-four chance that any child of ours would develop the condition. Coincidentally, Tom is the fourth of our four children.

But there is also another story of how this happened. It was my wife's desire for children, rather than mine, that brought our first three children into the world. Don't misunderstand me, I was very happy to go along with the idea and I love them all dearly. I just mean that the impetus was hers. In fact, I had never seriously thought about parenthood as something that I actively wanted until after our third child, Georgie, was born. She was just nine months old when for the first and only time in my life I found myself wanting to make a baby.

I can still remember the moment that Tom was conceived. I felt an extraordinary flood of energy pass through my body, quite unlike any other experience of love-making that I had known. I knew with a strange and absolute certainty that a new life had chosen to come into the world through me. Seven months later, Tom was born prematurely with - as I have often told him since - a smile on his face and a "copper seven" (an old-fashioned contraceptive device) in his right hand. Well, perhaps not actually in his hand. He weighed barely four pounds. His head was the size of an apple and I could hold him in the palms of my two hands. At first he had some breathing problems, as premature babies often do. His early months were punctuated by frequent trips to hospital but he survived them all. It seems that Tom is one of those souls who are determined to make the journey no matter how difficult.

I have never lost that deep sense of soul connection with Tom that began even before he was born. His being the youngest child also, I guess, meant that I paid him special attention. I especially loved physical contact, holding him close and feeling our hearts beating together. For several years during his early childhood (and for reasons completely unconnected with Tom) I suffered from depression and would spend hours each day just lying in bed. Often, when I was at my lowest, he would leave whatever game he was playing, sneak into the bedroom and silently snuggle down beside me soothing me with his presence until - in a touching reversal of roles - I would fall asleep and he would get up and return to his game.

He could be boisterous too, charging around at high speed, yelling at his brother and sisters, playing football, chasing the cats and laughing with the sheer delight of being alive. When he was about ten I took him on a fathers and sons weekend in North Wales. One morning, we stood on a shingly beach beside a stream making a boat out of old bits of wood and stuff. I scrabbled in the earth for some stones to ballast the boat and my hand fell upon a piece of slate in the shape of a twin heart. I held it up to show him. "Look Tom, it's us," I said.

He was unimpressed, refusing, as most ten year old boys would, to let himself be drawn into anything poetic. "That's soppy, Dad." Fifteen years later, I still have the piece of slate, propped up on my bookshelf. And I still think it's us.

Tom was a bright, intelligent youngster - tall for his age, gangling and (as we thought) just a bit more clumsy and awkward than most kids. Looking back, I feel quite ashamed at the number of times I told him "Look where you are going," or "Pull yourself together and stand up straight." Despite all this he seemed to have a remarkable level of emotional maturity. One day, after his mother and I separated when he was about thirteen, he telephoned me and said, "I'm really angry and upset with you Dad and I don't want to see you for a while. I'll let you know when I'm ready." Even though I was hurt by his words I was pleased and proud that he had been able to speak so clearly about his feelings. Six months later he called and said that he would like to see me again. After that, he often came to stay with me and we went on holiday together - including one memorable trip to Disneyland in Florida. I can still picture Tom's face after coming down the Space Mountain rollercoaster, speechless and with eyes as big as saucers from the speed and thrill of the curving, looping, pell-mell descent. One day, we even saw a real live space launch from Cape Canaveral: the shuttle and its booster rockets thundering into life, too loud to think, and even from a distance it seemed like everything was vibrating wildly as if we had been standing in the middle of an earthquake. Each evening we chose a different restaurant and ate in splendour, discussing the day's events like a couple of old gents dining at their club. It is a golden memory of a time before Tom's troubles really began, before the burden of his illness descended upon him.

Soon, his clumsiness became more pronounced and he began to fall over quite frequently. My ex-wife and I realised that there might be something seriously wrong and decided that we needed to find out for certain. It took us two years of going back and forth to doctors and consultants to get a diagnosis. By that time Tom had been on the internet and already worked out for himself that it was Friedreich's. Things have got gradually worse since then. Within a few years he couldn't walk unaided and now he can't stand by himself and needs a wheelchair all the time. Through all this, he has mostly kept his spirits up and never lost his wicked sense of humour. Although he is sometimes angry at his fate, he has never been bitter nor blamed us for his condition. In fact, he is incredibly generous and warm hearted, especially towards his brother and sisters. "I am just glad it's me and not one of them," he once said to me.

The four of them are still very close and it touches me deeply to see them together. I recall his sister, Georgie (now grown up and working in London), coming home and spending hours sitting on Tom's bed to keep him company, Jamie (now a great bear of a man) putting his arms round Tom to lift him bodily into his wheelchair, and Nicky (now a wife and mother of three small children) lifting her kids up onto Tom's bed so they could crawl all over him, much to his delight. He lives with his mum who looks after him and he is, in some mysterious way, the still centre around which our family, once so nearly broken by divorce, revolves.

Although the horizons of Tom's life have narrowed over the years, he has a young man's adventurous spirit that is determined to find expression. Back in 2003, for example, Tim (our daughter Nicky's husband) told me and my ex-wife that he wanted to do something for Tom. To cut a long story short, he and two friends did the Three Peaks Challenge, climbing the three highest mountains in Britain (Ben Nevis, Snowdon and Scafell Pike) in twenty-four hours to raise £3,000 to pay for Tom and his able-bodied friend Shaun to experience a ten day voyage around Antigua as crew members on the tall ship Tenacious. Because the ship is specially adapted for people with disabilities, Tom could take his turn preparing food, being on watch, and even being hoisted up the mast to the crow's nest in his wheelchair. I have a photograph of him at the helm with a broad smile on his face, the wind whipping at his sou'wester, his wheelchair strapped to the deck as the ship heels over in a lively breeze. Think "Pirates of the Caribbean" - complete with rolling seas, yards of billowing canvas, side-trips up steamy jungle rivers, and carousing in local bars - and you will be close.

I picked them up from Heathrow when they got back - two grubby, tired and very happy nineteen year olds. Tom reached out his arms to hug me. "Thanks, Dad," he said, "It was great." I looked into his eyes and could see that something had changed. He seemed somehow more self-confident and mature. "I'm very proud of you, Tom," I said, "You've done something most people never get to do. Welcome home."

These days Tom is less mobile and many of his adventures are conducted in cyber-space. He spends many hours playing online games. His favourite is called Final Fantasy; it's a multi-player, real-time adventure game played in teams. The players all have different characters that combine to search for treasure and kill monsters - well that's my limited understanding of it, I'm sure Tom would tell you that it's a lot more complicated than that. It gives him a world in which he can make friends and take his place alongside them as an equal and sometimes as a leader. As he said to me, "I am good at this game. It makes no difference that I am in a wheelchair. Inside here (tapping his head) I am as quick as a cat." I sometimes look over his shoulder when he is playing and I notice that the character he has chosen as his representative in this virtual world is not some mighty warrior but a quirky-looking healer with magic powers.

I began by saying that Tom is my hero and my greatest teacher in life. He is the bravest person I know. Despite the discomfort and limitations of his failing body he faces each new day with courage and equanimity. Recently he has moved into his own flat, specially adapted to meet his needs, and is thriving in a new and more independent life. His example shows me how to be grateful for small things and how to have fun in the face of adversity. Our games of backgammon (which he generally wins) have become notorious for our shrieks of laughter and bellowed profanities echoing through the house. When I spend time caring for him, looking after his physical needs, I have to adjust to match his pace and then he teaches me how to live one day at a time, moving through each day with a simpler, slower rhythm.

I read somewhere that love does not just break your heart, it breaks it open. There is no love without pain. When I can bear the pain of it, loving Tom opens my heart not just to him but to the wider world as well, bringing a greater sense of compassion for all our fragile, wounded selves. Tom touches the heart of everyone he meets and - though I would wish him a lighter burden and a different fate - I am immensely grateful for everything he has brought into my life and hugely proud of him, just as he is.

I finished speaking and sat quietly in the storyteller's chair, trembling slightly. I felt as though telling Tom's story had lifted a weight from my shoulders. The audience murmured their acknowledgement and some rubbed their hands together in silent applause. I saw many warm, supportive smiles as I returned to my seat amongst them and they wrote notes of appreciation for the story (as we had done earlier for the other stories). As they wrote, I reflected that I had been right to tell this story as simply as I could and not to craft some clever and elaborate tale. Right because it was the story and not the storyteller that mattered; right because the gifts Tom's life had brought me were gifts worth sharing.

Later, when I read the notes, I was touched by the impact of the story on some of the listeners and affirmed in my conviction that it had been the right story to tell. Someone wrote "This story really encourages us listeners to accept our destiny and be grateful for the gifts of life." Another said "Thank you, I hope you will continue to tell this story as in its telling your son continues to heal some part of all of us." Roi's note began "Just speak from the heart. Yes, I think that it is as simple and challenging as that. It is what makes a story a good story. Thank you for this courageous and heart-opening tale."

I put the notes down and recalled a favourite epigram from Ben Okri, one that I had often quoted but perhaps not fully understood before. "Maybe there are only three kinds of stories: the stories we live, the stories we tell, and the higher stories that help our souls fly up towards the greater light." Tom's story, I mused, encompassed all three. It was indeed a gift.

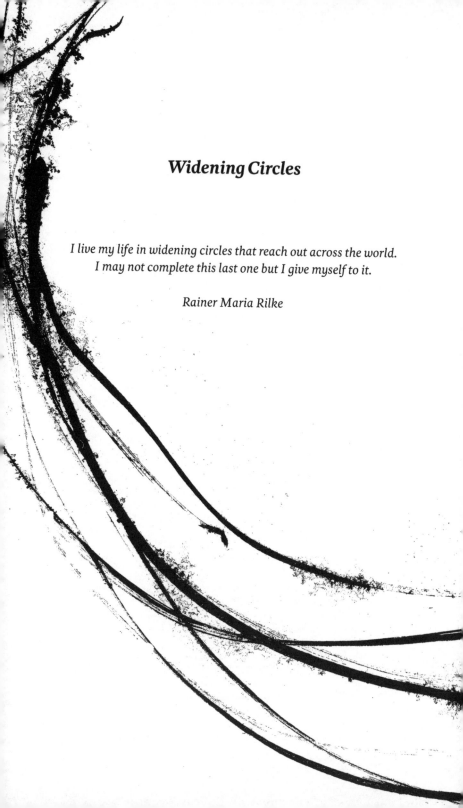

Widening Circles

*I live my life in widening circles that reach out across the world.
I may not complete this last one but I give myself to it.*

Rainer Maria Rilke

14
Some Enchanted Evening

To say that stories and storytelling can save the world would be a grandiose claim. Yet it seems that some stories and some kinds of storytelling are capable of speeding its destruction. To put it baldly, we might say that the myth of the industrial-growth society within which my generation has lived has led many of us - in the so-called developed world - to behave as though we believed that the planet's resources were infinite and that we were entitled to consume as many of them as possible (and produce as much waste as we liked in the process) without any significant consequences. So strong has been this tacit story that it has taken the tangible evidence of significant climate change, massive environmental degradation and a global economic crisis to begin to challenge its hegemony.

The way we are treating our home planet bespeaks a radical deracination, a profound loss of connection with our fellow humans and with the more-than-human world. The German sociologist Max Weber recognised this more than a century ago as a characteristic stance of *homo economicus*. He called it *die Entzauberung der Welt* - the disenchantment of the world. Instead of believing, as did our hunter-gatherer forbears and surviving indigenous peoples, that we intrinsically belong to and are part of an animate world, modern man (in shucking off mediaeval mysticism and feudal oppression) adopted the apparent rationality and objectivity of Cartesian philosophy and Newtonian science and the separation of Man from Nature that they both implied.

The notions that to be human is to participate in the whole of existence and that we are merely a part of and not the pinnacle of Creation, became largely disgraced. We gained the means of technological exploitation of our world and all the benefits that this has brought (for some at least) in terms of our material standard of living, medical and pharmaceutical developments, widespread literacy and access to education, greater social mobility and scope for individuality, to name but a few.

But the disenchantment of the world that accompanied this great enlightenment has also had unwelcome consequences: we fell out of love with the richness and glory of the natural world; we forgot about the importance of community and became dissociated from a sense of place; we paid less attention to the qualities of life than to the quantities of material goods we could accumulate; we lost respect for indigenous knowledge and the folk-wisdom of our own cultures.

Faced with such enormous challenges, how can we storytellers play a modest part in helping to mitigate some of these consequences? Perhaps one contribution we can make through our storytelling is towards the *reenchantment of the world*[38]. By reenchantment, I don't mean magical thinking or the naïve belief that wishing a thing makes it so. I mean a renewed awareness of our participation in the adventure of life and a deeper imagination of the significance of our actions.

Our stories can help to evoke a sense of wonder; they can allow animals and trees to speak and give voice to the silent world of rocks and mountains; they can put us back in touch with the seasons and the turning of the year; they bring the possibility of a more soulful connection with the communities and the places in which we live; they can celebrate the diversity and richness of many cultures and societies; they have the power to remind us of our history and our roots and thus - paradoxically - to understand that we have a responsibility towards the future. So it is not surprising that environmental campaigners such as David Abram (author of *Spell of the Sensuous* and *Becoming Animal*) and Stephan Harding (author of *Animate Earth*) are calling for a rejuvenation of oral culture as an ecological imperative:

...not to the exclusion of literate culture, nor to the exclusion of digital culture, but rather underneath these more abstract layers of society, providing their necessary soil and sustenance. For when left to itself, the literate intellect, adrift in the play of signs, easily forgets its dependence upon the body and the breathing earth - as the digital mind, dazzled by its own creations, often becomes oblivious to the sensuous surroundings.[39]

The stakes are high and it is easy to become dispirited and overwhelmed by the difficulties that surround us. It is so much easier to pretend that the difficulties do not exist or to believe that it is not worth doing anything because nothing we can do will make any difference. But we need not lose heart; it is better to make a modest contribution even if we cannot measure its effect. As ecological activist Joanna Macy says "We need not expect to see the results of our work: our actions have unanticipated and far-reaching effects that are not likely to be visible to us in our lifetime."[40] The work of storytellers is telling stories and, though we cannot know their ultimate effect, we can hope that in the right circumstances our storytelling helps bring people closer together and that our stories stimulate them to perceive the world in a more inclusive, enchanted way.

There is a wonderful story of this sort from Kazakhstan, called *The Magic Garden of the Poor*, that I often tell, sometimes to groups (in business and academia) who have asked me to help them think about living and working in more sustainable ways and sometimes in public performances (in storytelling clubs and festivals). It begins with two neighbours, a farmer and a shepherd, who are life-long friends. When the shepherd falls on hard times, the farmer gives him half his land. The shepherd finds a pot of gold buried in one of the fields he has been given and they quarrel good-naturedly when each tries to persuade the other to have it. Unlike so many stories, their dilemma springs not from greed but generosity; already it is inviting audiences to imagine the possibility of a world that operates more by collaboration rather than self-interest.

Unable to decide what to do, the two friends take the matter to the village headman who is at that moment teaching four students a lesson in the law. The fourth student (a young woman) offers her judgment in the same spirit of generosity:

When her turn comes, she says:"Since neither of them seems to want the gold for themselves, perhaps we could do some good with it. There are many people who have never smelt flowers or walked on green grass, have never eaten fresh fruit or sat in the cool shade of a tree or drunk clear fresh water. We could use the money to buy seeds and plants to make a garden for these poor people."

The farmer and the shepherd agree and the young woman is sent off to the capital city to buy the seeds and plants. None of these characters is well-off but they see the need to support those who have less than themselves - a chastening thought for those of us who have more than enough and live by a less communitarian ethos.

So far, the story has been confined to the human world but this changes when the young woman takes pity on a consignment of captive birds bound for the Khan's table and, instead of buying seeds and plants as she had undertaken to do, she uses the pot of gold to secure their release. She returns to the village empty-handed and weeps with despair because the garden for the poor can no longer be made. But the same birds that she had rescued overhear her plight and magically make the garden, which the poor can enjoy but is out of bounds to the rich and powerful.

The central characters in this story are motivated not by self-interest but by concern for each other and for the more-than-human world. It tells us that generosity is more rewarding than greed and that the surest way to receive is to give. The magic in the story comes from acting in the same spirit towards the birds, who represent the natural world. Surely, audiences are left to ponder, it is this spirit of mutual care that is the real pot of gold. We are not asked to believe the story but we are invited to believe in what it represents.

It is a sweet tale that, in my experience, never fails to engage and provoke thoughtful reactions from audiences of all types and ages. A full version of *The Magic Garden of the Poor* follows this chapter.

But we need not visit the exotic wastes of Kazakhstan to experience the way storytelling can help to reenchant the world. Indeed there is something precious about bringing storytelling closer to home, to the communities of which we are a part. Although I travel widely and the stories I tell come from all over the world, my ancestry is English. My roots are in England; its heritage and traditions are in my blood. It is my home and if I want to use my storytelling to make a difference in the world then I must begin here with the people I know in the land that I love.

One of the ways that I have tried to do this is by putting on local storytelling performances at Christmastime. Even in our comfortable, centrally-heated, electrically-lit corner of the world, there is something about the depth of winter that draws people together in search of companionship and community. It is a time of year when people share food and drink with their neighbours and families, when they talk about the old year and look forward to the new. It is also, as I have discovered, a time when storytellers are particularly welcomed into village halls, community centres, farmhouses and homes up and down the country to tell seasonal tales.

Perhaps that shouldn't be a surprise. After all, midwinter festivals have been celebrated by people from many different cultures[41] from time immemorial, to mark the turning of the year as the nights begin to shorten and to bring light and warmth to the coldest, darkest time of the year. Each year it delights me - and my partner Chris - to respond to invitations or put ourselves forward to give a storytelling performance or two just before Christmas. Looking back at nearly a decade of telling seasonal stories together at such venues as Grimstone Manor (a centre for personal development courses and workshops), church halls and village halls (including Chris's home village, Kingscote), and once at a remote Welsh farmhouse in Cilycwm, I think it is possible to get a good sense of what our storytelling brought to these very different communities.

We were always warmly thanked (and usually collected a small donation for some local charity) but the most heart-warming thing was the way audiences hung around afterwards, exchanging greetings and chatting with each other, apparently reluctant to leave. It seemed as though the distances between people had shrunk, as though - for the moment, at least - they were more conscious and appreciative of being in community. The shared experience of listening to the stories had brought them closer together.

There are many memorable moments from those evenings that I could use to illustrate my point but a handful will suffice. I vividly recall, for example, the sheer joy and raucous delight of the audience at Kingscote Village Hall as they provided the sound effects and actions for Chris's telling of *The Queen with the Cold, Cold Heart*.

The handsome young prince [cries of "Aha!" with right fists raised in the air] galloped on his milk white steed [whinnying and the sound of hands slapping thighs for galloping hooves] past the first princess who had a dreadful cold [fingers drawn across nostrils and loud sniffing], past the second princess who had a bad chest [coughing sounds, shoulders slumped], past the third princess who was beautiful but sad [soft "Aaaaah" with head tilted to one side] until he stopped in front of the palace guard ["Halt! Who goes there?"]

And so on. Friends and neighbours in the audience yelled outrageously, waved their arms and laughed out loud as they joined in the story, making fools of themselves together and evidently enjoying the process.

Sometimes the stories were more serious and poignant and they too served to bring people together. One year, at Grimstone Manor, I told a story set during the Second World War about two elderly strangers (a Jew and a Christian) telling tales of better times to keep warm as they sheltered in a ramshackle hut in the forest in the snowy depths of winter. They share memories of Christmas and Hanukkah gifts and celebrations with their families before the war and then make up a story about how an impoverished young couple, in a similarly war-torn country, had discovered that the only gift worth giving or receiving was their love for each other.

And as their story ended and the first light of day crept into the room, the old man and the old woman realised that it was silent outside. The gunfire had stopped. They stood up slowly and the old man pushed open the door. The sky was clear and they watched as the rising sun glinted off fresh snowflakes, so that they sparkled like diamonds amongst the trees. They hugged briefly then made their separate ways out into the world through that chill winter landscape... warmed by the story they carried within them.

As I told the story (and the story within the story) I looked round the room and saw lots of moist eyes and tears running down some people's cheeks.

Some listeners had reached out to join hands with those sitting beside them or to put an arm around their shoulders. Their shared compassion for the characters in the story was palpable and very moving.

At the farmhouse at Cilycwm, we slipped in a couple of short scary stories amongst the usual seasonal fare.

The girl didn't like being on her own in that big old house. She decided to go to bed early. She locked her bedroom door, changed into her nightdress and then - just to make sure - she looked in the wardrobe and the chest of drawers and even under her bed. Then she got in, pulled the covers up tight and turned out the light. "That's good," said a quiet voice. "We're safely locked in for the night."

Sitting by the hearth, we looked out at round-eyed children staring back, faces rosy in the firelight, scrunching deeper into their parents' and grandparents' laps and squealing in mock horror at the punch lines.

Over the years we told a wide range of stories from around the world: tales of the Golden Buddha from Thailand, a traveller's tale from Scotland of the scarecrow that went to the Christmas party, a trickster story from the plains of Kazakhstan, a snowy Japanese romance, an alternative Russian nativity, a foolish tale from the Appalachians involving Santa Claus and a candle that wouldn't blow out, and many more besides. Each evening was unique and yet their effect on the groups of people who came to them was similar.

What they had in common, I think, was that hearing the stories enabled people safely to experience and express a wide range of emotions, including ones that might not usually be socially acceptable like fear, sorrow, and anger as well as surprise, wonder, compassion and joy. Bringing these frequently private emotions into a sanctioned public space is one way people are healed, groups become communities and communities are strengthened.

Such a claim is not new. Aristotle wrote over two millennia ago about the social benefits of *methexis* (group sharing) and *catharsis* (emotional release) in ancient Greek drama[42]. Storytelling, too, is a kind of theatre (with the storyteller's chair as the stage). Indeed, it probably provides the human species' oldest form of drama. Add to that the ritual of sharing food and drink as part of a midwinter festival, the need for which seems to be located deep in the human psyche, and you have a powerful recipe for community-building.

At Grimstone Manor, we were telling to a temporary, albeit intimate, community - a group of strangers who would only be together for a week or two then disperse. Here, perhaps, we were helping to create a sense of community amongst a disparate group. Kingscote Village, on the other hand, had a more settled, long-term community but one that was only loosely associated, with relatively infrequent social contact between neighbours. Here, I think, our performances helped to affirm and deepen an existing, though latent, sense of community. The farmhouse at Cilycwm, enjoying the best of both worlds, brought several generations of families, old friends and close neighbours together for our performance - a small community of people that was both intimate and enduring. Here, it seems, our evening of seasonal storytelling helped people to celebrate the deep bonds of family and friendship that were already firmly in place.

There is no reason to think that Christmas is the only time of year when storytelling can do its magic. Each season calls for its own tales - and many can be enjoyed at any time at all - but I do have a particular fondness for the stories and storytelling of mid-winter. Like most of humankind, I too yearn for light in the midst of darkness and crave warmth to keep me from the cold. Thinking of those evenings at Grimstone and Kingscote and Cilycwm, it occurs to me that we storytellers are fire-bringers; our stories spark the imagination and ignite the emotions. No wonder there is a place for us at the hearth when it is cold and dark outside - we are carrying a torch for an ancient and honourable tradition.

Who would disagree that the magic of storytelling is an essential and timely contribution to the reenchantment of our disenchanted world, a necessary and enjoyable way of bringing people together to strengthen our sense of connection with each other and with the places where we live, and a route to imagining ourselves once more as whole-hearted participants in a wider circle of Creation with all the blessings and responsibilities that brings.

The Magic Garden of the Poor

Once, there were two neighbours who were great friends. One was a farmer and the other was a shepherd. The farmer lived and worked on a small but fertile plot of land in the valley-bottom and the shepherd cared for his flocks on the stony upper slopes above the farm. They had known each other since boyhood and not once had they exchanged a cross word.

One day a terrible disease struck the shepherd's flocks. The sheep sickened and died. With no sheep left to care for, the shepherd went to say goodbye to his friend. "Why must you go?" asked the farmer.

"I cannot afford to replace my flock," said the shepherd. "I will have to live in the town and take some sort of menial job or perhaps even beg to make a living."

"I won't hear of it," said the farmer. "You are my friend. Stay here with me, I have enough land for both of us. I will give you half my fields."

"You have little enough already," said the shepherd. "Besides, I don't now how to grow things. You are very kind but I must go."

"I won't hear of it," said the farmer. "There is enough land for us both if we are careful and I will teach you how to be a farmer. Please stay. How could I enjoy my life without you?"

So the shepherd agreed. The farmer gave him half his land, helped him build a small house and - season by season - taught him how to grow and harvest crops. Things went on like this for some years and the friends were very happy to live so close to each other and see each other so often. Then, one day, as the shepherd was clearing the corner of a field that was thick with weeds, his mattock went deep into the earth and he heard a clang. When he delved down to see what his implement had struck, he found a pot full of gold coins. Excited, he dug it out of the ground and rushed to show his friend the farmer.

"Look what I have found," said the shepherd. "You are rich."

"What do you mean, I am rich?" replied the farmer. "You found

170

the gold. I gave you the land. The gold is yours."

"Of course it isn't," said the shepherd. "You did not know that there was gold buried there when you gave me the land. The gold is yours."

Each continued in the same way, trying to persuade the other to have the gold and - for the first time in their lives - they began to argue. Soon, though, they called a halt to their quarrel. "It is clear that we can't decide who should have the gold," said the farmer. "Let's go and ask the village headman what we should do."

The shepherd agreed and the two men walked the few miles from where they lived to the village. When they got there, they found the headman sitting in the sun-bleached square with four young students to whom he was teaching the law. They showed the pot of gold to the headman and his students and told them what had happened. "So we have come to ask you what we should do," they said together when they had finished their story.

The headman thought this would be an excellent case for his students to consider. He turned to the first student and asked him what he thought should be done. The young man scratched his head and said, "The gold was found in the ground. If they cannot decide whose it is then I think they should bury it again and leave it there."

The headman tutted and turned to the second student. "And what is your opinion?" This young man thought for a while and then said with a smile, "If they cannot decide what to do with the gold, perhaps they should give it to us."

The headman frowned and turned to the third young man. "They found the gold in the ground," said this student. "The ground is part of the land and surely the land and everything in it truly belongs to the Khan who rules us all. I think they should take the gold and give it to the Khan."

But this answer did not please the headman any more than those he had heard already and he scowled angrily. "I hope you can come up with a better idea than these three," he said to the fourth student, a young woman. "I do have an idea," she said nervously. "Since neither of them seems to want the gold for themselves, perhaps we could do some good with it. There are many people who have never smelt flowers or walked on green grass, have never eaten fresh fruit or sat in the cool shade of a tree or drunk clear fresh water. We could use the money to buy seeds and plants to make a garden for these poor people."

This time the headman smiled. He turned towards the shepherd and the farmer who were both nodding their heads. "We like her idea," they said, handing the pot of gold to the fourth student. "And we think she is just the person to take the gold and buy the seeds and plants."

"I didn't mean me," said the young woman. "I wouldn't know where to get them. Someone else should do it."

"It was your idea and it seems that you have been chosen," said the headman. "You will have to go to the market in the capital city. It is far away but you are young and strong and I am sure that you can do it. There is a piece of land just outside our village that nobody uses and that is where the garden shall be made. It is all decided. Now, off you go."

So the young woman made the long journey on foot to the capital city where the Great Khan had his palace. The road was hot and dusty, the way was hard but the dream of a garden for the poor kept her going when she was tired and thirsty. A week after she had set off, she arrived in the outskirts of the city. She had never been there before, in fact she had never been to any city before and she was stunned by the opulence of the tightly-packed stone houses and the bustling streets full of people coming and going. Drivers whipped at donkeys pulling carts piled high with pots and pans, sacks of food and rolls of carpet. Everywhere she went, traders and merchants called out their wares, tempting passers-by to stop and haggle.

The young woman walked on, gazing in wonder at the brilliant colours in the dye-market and filling her nostrils with the myriad pungent aromas from the spice-sellers' stalls. It took her some time to find the stalls that sold seeds and plants but once there she diligently examined every item and picked out the very finest specimens. She had just finished gathering them all together and was about to pay for them when there was a terrific commotion. A camel train had entered the market and was forcing its way though the crowd, pushing people aside and scattering goods from the stalls.

As it drew closer she saw a horrid sight: hanging from the camels, suspended by strings attached to their feet, were scores of live birds. With each step the sorry creatures banged against the flanks of the camels and dust billowed from their shabby plumage. Tears of pity sprang from her eyes and she felt her heart rise up into her throat. Without thinking, the young woman stepped out in front of the leading camel. "Stop!" she shouted to the camel driver. "Where are you going with these birds?"

The camel train lurched to a halt. "They are for the Great Khan himself," said the camel driver. "Not that it is any of your business. Their meat will grace his table and the feathers will decorate the walls of his palace. These birds have been collected from the four corners of the kingdom. They are the rarest and most beautiful birds to be found anywhere; some of them are the last of their kind. Now, get out of my way."

"I will buy them from you," said the young woman. The words leapt unbidden from her mouth. "I have gold. I will buy them from you."

"You would need a lot of gold to buy these," said the camel driver. "I have already been promised a good price."

"I have a whole pot of gold," the young woman replied, holding it out in both hands in front of her. The camel driver got down and counted the gold coins. It was more than even the Great Khan would have paid him for his cargo. He pocketed the money and the young woman untied the birds. Those that were able to use their wings flew off at once. Those that were too dazed and bedraggled to fly she put at the side of the road. When all the birds had been released, she stroked the dust from the sickly ones and gently massaged their bodies, speaking to them softly. All day she worked until one by one they flapped their wings and flew away. She felt good about what she had done but now she had no gold to pay for the seeds and plants so she made her way out of the city to begin the long walk home, empty-handed.

The further she went, the more she began to doubt her actions. By the time she had got close to the village, the thought of explaining what she had done to the headman and to the shepherd and the farmer was almost more than she could bear. She sat down on the ground - by chance on the very spot where the headman had decided that the garden would be made - and wept. "I could not let those poor birds suffer but the gold was not mine to give and now there will be no garden for the poor," she said aloud.

Just then she noticed a robin on the ground beside her. Its head was cocked to one side and it looked straight at her as if listening to her words. It suddenly flew off but returned almost immediately. Soon the air was filled with the sound of birds' wings and a multitude of different birds - finches and thrushes, eagles and doves, parrots and parakeets, buzzards and owls, blackbirds and birds of paradise, in fact all manner of birds that you could think of - circled around the young woman's head before alighting in front of her. The robin cocked its head to one side and spoke.

"Do not cry. You saved us and now it is our turn to help you. We cannot give you back the gold you used to free us but we can help you make the garden you dream of."

The smaller birds began to peck at the ground, loosening the soil. They rolled the pebbles and stones out of the way while the larger birds flew off to the four corners of the kingdom and beyond to fill their beaks with the most precious seeds and shoots they could find. When they returned, the birds planted the seeds and then flew to a nearby stream to bring water. Then they dug ponds and the eagles flew far off to the high mountains to bring back clear fresh water to fill them.

As the young woman watched, the birds fanned the seeds with their wings and blew on them with their hot breath. Before her eyes, the seeds sprouted and their shoots quickly began to grow. Some spread out to become a lush green lawn of grass; some pushed up higher and became flowers that opened their blooms to release their intoxicating scent; others grew higher still into trees that budded and blossomed and hung heavy with apples.

News of the amazing garden spread quicker than a hare can run. Of course, the rich and the powerful assumed that it was meant for them and they soon turned up on their fine horses to investigate this new wonder and to see what was in it for them. But when they arrived in the middle of the day, they found that a stone wall had sprung up around the garden. The stone wall had an iron gate and the iron gate had seven locks which locked themselves as the men on horseback approached. There was no way they could get into the garden. One of them stood in his saddle and reached over the wall to pluck a juicy golden apple but when he touched it he felt a shock as though he had been struck by lightning. "This is some peasant magic," said the horsemen. "There is nothing here worth having." And they rode off back to wherever they had come from.

By late afternoon, poor people began to arrive from all directions. A host of men, women and children shuffled in their tattered clothes towards the garden. Many were barefoot and all were tired, hungry and thirsty. As they approached, the seven locks unlatched themselves and the iron gate swung open to welcome them. Wide-eyed with wonder, they entered the garden. They smelt the heady scent of the flowers, felt the soft green grass push between their toes and drank deep draughts of the clear fresh water from the ponds. They reached up and plucked some of the luscious apples and ate them, juice streaming down their chins. Then they sat with their backs against the trees and took their ease in the shade, talking and laughing with delight.

When dusk came, most returned home but those with nowhere to go wrapped their rags around them and lay down on the grass to sleep. The iron gate swung shut and the seven locks locked themselves to keep the visitors safe from harm.

The story says nothing more about the young woman whose dream the garden was, nor about the farmer and the shepherd whose gold she used to release the birds. It simply tells us that as night fell in the garden of the poor, the apples that hung from the trees glowed and bathed the sleepers with a soft blue light and the birds settled in the branches and sang a sweet lullaby.

About the story

This is a Kazakh folktale which appears in Margaret Read Macdonald's book *Earth Care: World Folktales To Talk About* (published by August House, Arkansas in 1999). She adapted it from earlier sources and the version that appears here is quite true to her delightful original though I have re-written it to reflect the language I use when telling it as an oral story. One significant change I have made is to make the fourth student a young woman because doing so implicitly reinforces the idea that we need to stop behaving on the basis of patriarchal consciousness. In my experience, the story's touching themes of friendship, generosity and care for both the human and the more-than-human world never fail to delight audiences of all ages.

15
Storytelling in Organisations

Nowhere is the disenchantment of the world more evident than in the impersonal and target-driven behaviours of the organisations that dominate our society: large-scale corporations, government departments, universities and educational institutions, even health and social care providers. That is not to accuse either the organisations or the people working in them of being evil or malicious. On the whole, I assume that both are well-intentioned and do their best within the frames of reference within which they operate.

Nevertheless, there often seems to be a huge gulf between the ways in which we are required to behave (or believe we are required to behave) in the complex systems of the modern age and the things that concern us in our everyday human lives: domains that sociologist Jurgen Habermas called the system-world and the life-world.[43]

The place of storytelling in the life-world is easy to recognise. Indeed, almost everything written in the preceding chapters of this book is located in that domain. Yet, if we storytellers are truly to play our part in what has been described as the reenchantment of the world, then we cannot afford to stand aloof from the system-world where the collective disenchantment of our society is most deeply embedded. How can storytelling make a difference in this domain? If we go a little bit deeper into Habermas's ideas we will find a clue.

He argued that the system-world and the life-world have become decoupled in our industrial and post-industrial societies, as though we believed that our working lives and our non-working lives were quite unconnected. What is more, he says, the economic power and efficiency of the system-world are such that the end-driven logic that underpins its success has a propensity to overwhelm the more communitarian logic of the life-world. Put another way: the short-term achievement of economic goals generally trumps the long-term consideration of our human needs (including our relationship with the more-than-human world).

If this apparently inexorable trend is to be reversed then we must find ways to reconnect the two worlds and to reassert the primacy of the life-world. The first step is to create what Habermas called communicative spaces where we can try to bridge the gulf between the two domains: opportunities for people in organisations to come together on equal terms to share what really matters to them as living, loving, struggling human beings, who are part of and not separate from the systems in which they work. And this is exactly where the quintessentially human phenomenon of storytelling comes in.

We can tell traditional stories that help individuals connect with archetypal and universal human themes; we can help people deepen their relationships and build their sense of community by enabling them to tell their own stories to each other; we can assist those in leadership roles to tell stories that describe and explain what is going on in more personal and human ways. In fact, once you begin to think about it, the possibilities for storytelling in organisations are endless. Although, as the following stories of some my own attempts to bring storytelling into a variety of organisational settings reveal, working as a storyteller in the system-world demands a hard-won understanding of how organisations work as well as a passion for story.

Even as I embarked on my personal journey as a storyteller, I began to look for opportunities to bring storytelling into my professional practice as an organisational consultant (work that I began alongside my police career in the 1990s when I was seconded to a consulting firm for six months). At first I approached this with what now looks to me like a rather touching naiveté. It all seemed so obvious and I was so excited by the idea of storytelling that my enthusiasm sometimes got the better of me. I recall dropping in stories and story games (such as story tag where a spontaneous story is created and passed from person to person) into team-building sessions and telling one of the few stories I knew whenever I could make the slightest connection with the work in hand. It is not surprising that sometimes eyebrows were raised and people looked puzzled. Nowadays, I'm slightly embarrassed to think that my watchword as a consultant at that time could well be caricatured as "Story is the answer. Now, what is your problem?"

However I persisted and began to notice that sometimes, after telling a traditional story, the nature of the conversation would change. It became more expansive and inclusive and seemed to allow people to bring more of themselves into the room. I once told the story of *Jumping Mouse*[44] to a group of organisational consultants whose "away day" I had been asked to facilitate. After I finished the story they commented on the images they had particularly noticed in the tale and some of the similarities between the obstacles faced by its hero and challenges in their own work. Then gradually, almost imperceptibly, more personal stories emerged. They spoke about their children and about when they had been children themselves. They recalled times when as infants they had been told stories by their parents, grandparents or by a beloved aunt or uncle. I noticed some of their eyes glisten with joyful or poignant memories. The quality of the group's breathing changed as though they had released a collective outbreath, a silent sigh as they settled into a deeper level of being before moving on to the business of the day.

There was an optimistic simplicity to my approach that served well enough for a while but I soon hit the limits of what I could do because at that time I did not really understand the power of story myself. Oliver Wendell Holmes once said, "I don't give a fig for the simplicity this side of complexity, but I would die for the simplicity on the other side." My original approach was simple (and simplistic) because I had not yet begun to wrestle with the depth and complexity of storytelling. I had not yet understood or done enough to earn the simplicity on the other side.

Challenging myself to go further, I started to offer workshops on storytelling and leadership. I began tentatively to explore new ways of bringing story into organisations and working with the human stories that were already there. By some mysterious process, word got out and a steady trickle of curious (not to say adventurous) clients contacted me to ask if I would come and do something with storytelling. They gave me the chance to hone my thinking about the ways in which story works and pushed me into developing my practice to meet their needs. I soon became adept at getting all sorts of people in organisations to share their personal stories of successes and failures with each other. Often this resulted in the kind of deepening of relationships that I had been asked to help them achieve. But sometimes it didn't work so well. Occasionally some people were reticent to speak or found it difficult to make themselves heard in the group, whilst others seemed overly fond of the sound of their own voices.

Whenever this kind of thing happened, the results were disappointing. Instead of opening up new possibilities for relating to each other on a more equal footing (as I had intended), we merely replicated - or even reinforced - the existing power-based dynamic in the group. After a while, I realised that to get consistently positive results, I needed to find a form of sharing in which power and voice would be equalised as far as possible and in which all participants would be supported to tell their stories and to listen with equal attention to the stories of others.

While I was wrestling with this problem I happened to go to a conference at which a consultant, Theresa Holden, was running a session on the use of "story circles". She and her colleagues at Holden Arts (working in the field of conflict resolution and community-building in North America) had taken the basic idea of sitting in a circle and telling stories and developed it into a deceptively simple (on the other side of complexity) form in which each participant has equal opportunity and time to tell a story on a particular theme - and to be heard without interruption. The method had its roots in the Native American tradition of speaking in a circle and passing round a "talking stick" to denote the speaker's right to an audience, although we would limit each person's time and use a wristwatch instead of a stick. We tried it out at the conference and I was immediately impressed. It seemed to be exactly what I was looking for.

Since then I have used the process many times and discovered that it is incredibly robust and reliable. One example of how well the story circle technique can work for clients occurred a few years ago, with a group of fourteen engineers, members of a fast-track management training scheme in a large aerospace company. Working in two story circles, they each told stories in response to the trigger "Tell a three minute story about an event, a person, a moment or memory of a time that helped bring you to your work today for XYZ Company." They told of mentors in the company who had helped them, of inspired school teachers who had encouraged them to become engineers, of following in the footsteps of parents and grandparents, of breaking the mould to become the first person in their families to go to university, and of being one of relatively few women engineers in the company. There were stories of their hopes, doubts, fears and gratitude for the opportunities they had been given. Some were "natural" storytellers, some were a bit vague and lacking in detail, some artful, others artless but all had a story to tell and all were heard by their colleagues with rapt attention.

Afterwards, one of them said in tones that suggested a sense of wonder, "We really opened up to each other didn't we? We all work in the same business and we have been together on this training scheme for two years but I look round the room now and for the first time I feel that I actually know these people and that they know me."

Telling our stories to each other and listening to each other's stories are ways in which we express our sense of belonging to a particular community, society or nation. When we do not value each other in this way, when the stories of one part of a group has no currency with another part of a group it is a significant symptom of division. Wise leaders know this and also appreciate the possibility of taking action to heal such divisions. A year after Nelson Mandela became the first post-apartheid President of South Africa, he established the Truth and Reconciliation Commission, by means of which both victims and perpetrators - whether black or white - of abuses and injustices in the apartheid years could tell their stories and be listened to. The basis of the Commission was neither retribution nor conviction for past misdemeanours but the possibility of healing that comes from speaking the truth and valuing the stories - no matter how painful - of those from all sides of the age-old racial conflict. It is just one example of a process that has proved its efficacy in the wake of even the most troubled times.[45] I sometimes tell the story of the Commission to organisational leaders and ask them "Whose stories don't get heard in your organisation?" Quite often they will then ask me for a set of guidelines so they can start running story-circles themselves.

In the past few years, much of my work has been about storytelling in organisations. It ranges from running introductory, day-long, open workshops to working within long-term client relationships and includes such things as speaking at conferences, coaching chief executives and senior managers, diagnostic interventions and culture change, in-house team development, scenario building and strategy development, staff engagement and communication. In other words, I do the usual stock-in-trade of organisational consulting but all with a specific and explicit focus on storytelling and the effective and ethical use of story and narrative.

A particular highlight of my work has come when clients have asked me to work intensively with leaders in their organisations to help them tell their stories well. Not manufactured "spin", but authentic stories coming from personal experience that carry weight and the "ring of truth", stories that help them claim their personal authority, ones that inspire and engage people in service of worthwhile ends.

Once, for example, I was contracted to work with the chief executive of a national retail chain. Let us call her Jane. Faced for the first time in the company's history with something other than continuous growth and rising profits to report, Jane had felt at a loss as to how to talk with staff about the coming year. Used to relying on rising sales figures to speak for themselves, she knew that something else was needed but was unsure exactly what to do. What emerged from our coaching sessions was the awareness that she had to come out from behind the statistics, allow herself to be seen and tell it like it was.

So this time, when Jane stood up in front of the staff in the canteen at company headquarters she began very differently from the way she had always begun before.

Well, it has been a tough year. I don't know about you but I am feeling rather windswept and storm-tossed. I want to talk to you about why it has been tough when we are so used to success, what we are already doing about it and the key things we will all need to focus on in the next twelve months.

The image of a storm had prompted thoughts of a story Jane could tell to make her message memorable.

I am not a sailor myself but when I look ahead to next year it makes me think about someone who is. Yachtswoman Dee Caffari has already sailed single-handedly round the world and now she is preparing to do it all over again. But this time she is going the other way around. This time the prevailing winds and tides will not be in her favour. If she is going to succeed, her boat has to be in tip-top condition, she has to stay absolutely focused and she has to trust all the people in her team on shore. And that is just how we need to be because the going will be tough for us too next year. We are doing everything we can to make sure our ship is in the best possible shape and I am confident that we can do it.

It sounds pretty straightforward, perhaps even a bit trite, when I write it down. But no-one who saw Jane stand there, looking her staff in the eyes, her courage and determination to succeed on display, is likely to forget the experience. The story was good enough and told well enough to hit the mark but what really mattered was that telling it was a way for Jane herself to become more present. It also provided a powerful image that her listeners could identify with: getting their "boat" in good order because they faced a tough voyage against the prevailing economic winds and tides. Whatever happened in that room happened in the space between the teller and the listeners, a space where the honesty and vulnerability, rather than the skill, of the teller are what really count.

As someone who spent thirty years working as a public servant, I have also very much enjoyed bringing storytelling into government departments and other public sector organisations which often communicate their important messages in a rather dry and dusty way. Recently I have been commissioned by the Cabinet Office and the National School of Government to run workshops to teach top civil servants about the potential of storytelling to help them connect with the public and with their staff and stakeholders more effectively. Sometimes I have been able to talk with participants after these workshops to see what use they make of their newly-learned storytelling skills. I was particularly touched by a conversation in June 2009 with Ben Dyson, a senior official in the Department of Health, a few weeks after I had run a storytelling workshop he had attended on the Top Management Programme.

He told me that he had been invited to address a group of fifty Department of Health officials about the importance of equality and diversity issues when treating patients in the National Health Service and had decided to tell a story to make his point. I asked him to tell me the story just as he had told them. "Well," he said, "It's a true story. It's in the public domain now because there was a public inquiry. I said something like this."

A few years ago, a man - let's call him Michael - was admitted to hospital after he had a stroke. Michael was 43 years old and had severe learning disabilities. He had difficulty communicating with people he was not familiar with or making his needs known. The stroke had left him unable to swallow but somehow the medical team did not make a decision about alternative feeding until he had been in hospital for 18 days. Soon after that, Michael became too ill to undergo the procedure to insert a feeding tube and he subsequently died. His parents complained that he had, in effect, been "starved to death" whilst in the care of the National Heath Service. I very much doubt if any of those doctors or nurses charged with looking after Michael went into work wanting to provide sub-standard care. If they had been challenged they would have said "Of course we provide good quality care for everyone." So how did we - the system - let Michael and his parents down so badly?

I asked Ben how the story had gone down with his audience and he told me that instead of looking down at their note-books as so often happened at these events, they had been on the edge of their seats. "They were looking straight at me and leaning forward as if they wanted to know more. There were looks of surprise and I had a sense of light bulbs suddenly being switched on, as if they were saying to themselves 'Ah yes. That's what equalities issues are all about'. Afterwards, people came up to me and said how struck they had been by the story I had told."

I asked Ben how he had felt as he told the story and his reply seemed to confirm everything I had said in the workshop about our innate capacity to tell stories. "Initially, I felt a bit nervous because I normally don't tell stories and I was trying this out for real. But when I got into the rhythm of telling the story I found that I actually relaxed more than if I hadn't been telling a story. It occurs to me that recounting company policy is not something we learned in the nursery but the rhythms and cadences of a story are. It was a lot easier to do than I had imagined it would be."

Moments like this bring home to me both how important and how rewarding it can be to sprinkle the water of human stories onto the sometimes parched landscapes of our organisations.

The movement of my work towards organisational storytelling has accelerated in recent years but the path has been long and not always smooth. I have sometimes found it difficult, despite how strongly I believe in the power of story, to trust that it will earn me a living. It has been hard to turn away other kinds of work to leave space for story work to emerge. At times I have looked anxiously at my cash flow and sometimes grabbed at opportunities for more conventional consulting work to make sure I have enough money to pay the bills. Despite these hiccups, I take great satisfaction from the work itself, which is usually good, sometimes great and generally directed towards helping decent people do difficult and honourable things.

I have no doubt that the organisational storytelling practices described in this chapter can help to reconnect the *life-world* and the *system-world* and that they can reassert the primacy of human needs and the needs of the more-than-human world. But stories are powerful and not necessarily benign. The potential of storytelling to enchant can be misused as so-called "spin-doctors" and propagandists know only too well. Organisational storytellers must tread carefully to ensure that their efforts are not co-opted by the *system-world* to create monolithic organisational stories that leave no room for dissent or diversity. What organisations need is akin to what the planet needs: a healthy ecology of stories that enables the people in them (and the environment surrounding them) to thrive.

16
Water on the Rock

The second decade of the twenty-first century is undoubtedly an exciting and formative time to be involved with storytelling in organisations: a time when it is possible to influence developments in an emerging field of practice - just the kind of time I love. But alongside rapidly-growing interest amongst clients, consultants, coaches, storytellers and researchers - all encouraging signs that storytelling in organisations is an idea whose time has come - I began to notice a few years ago some isolated warning signs and signals that the shadow side of taking storytelling and the power of stories into organisations was also beginning to manifest. A couple of clients asked me to create simplistic corporate propaganda stories. Academic researchers by the dozen - eschewing practice for theory - began turning out weighty, dull publications that stripped all the life out of the subject. Licensed storytelling methodologies and associated commercial accreditation courses for storytelling practitioners started to appear. Some storytellers with little or no organisational experience (and some organisational consultants with little or no understanding of story) chose to market themselves as experts in organisational storytelling.

Looking back on these events in the light of the ideas of Jurgen Habermas that were explored in the previous chapter, they seem to constitute an example of what he called the *colonisation* of the *life-world* by the *system-world*: the tendency in our modern society for the formalisation, exploitation and control of the stuff of everyday life. At the time, however, as I slowly pieced these phenomena together, the story that unfolded in my mind was that I was witnessing the confused and unseemly scrabble of frontier life. A few explorers were opening up a new arena whilst others staked out and claimed ownership of territory, exploited the gullibility of the innocent and sought the riches of a potential gold rush. Inevitably some people sought to establish their control of the frontier under the guise of bringing order to the Wild West.

I had already twice experienced, at first hand, the desire of the *system-world* to regulate and control new forms of practice and systematise new knowledge in areas in which I had been deeply involved (Gestalt psychology and personal coaching) in the 1980s and 1990s. In my view, fields that had been incredibly exciting and creative in their early stages quickly became stultified by over-regulation, over-theorisation and over-exploitation. In hindsight, I could see that that was precisely why I had left them behind, preferring to explore other new frontiers. I had no desire to see storytelling in organisations (much less storytelling in general) follow the same route. This time, I decided, it would not be enough to explore this frontier and move on. This time, I would do something - though I didn't know what - to champion and preserve the beauty, freedom and diversity of a territory that had become my home and that I already knew would be my final resting place.

Things came to a head early in 2007 when I heard storyteller Hugh Lupton and musician Chris Wood give an extraordinary performance of a new work, On Common Ground based on the life of the nineteenth century Northamptonshire "peasant poet", John Clare. Born the son of "commoners" and sharing his early life with them close to the soil in an open landscape without hedges and fences, Clare - a sensitive soul - was tormented by the privatisation and parcelling up of the countryside that followed the Enclosure Acts and spent the last twenty-seven years of his life in asylums for the insane. As I listened to this poignant story unfold, it struck me how the same pernicious tendency to enclose and claim ownership of public property had extended into so many aspects of our lives in the twenty-first century, from intellectual property to specific human genes. What would come next - *Storytelling* ™ ?

I have no qualms about people legitimately enjoying

the fruits of their labour as storytellers, but the prospect of drifting into a world in which we would be excluded from our shared human heritage of stories and storytelling seemed only too real as I pondered the life and poetry of John Clare and wondered how I could help to preserve the storytelling commons.

In the days and weeks that followed, I began to think about what sort of contribution I could make to develop the field of storytelling in organisations in a healthy way. The more I thought about it, the more problematic the whole issue became. For a start, taking storytelling into organisations at all had thrown up some serious moral and personal dilemmas. I recalled a recent occasion when a colleague and I had been asked to deliver a series of workshops for groups of senior partners from a large professional services company. Our brief had been to teach them some storytelling techniques to help them engage with their clients in a more personal and memorable way. It sounded quite straightforward and the pay was good. We eagerly accepted the invitation and went along to a smart business school for the first workshop.

The trouble began as soon as a managing partner arrived to talk to the group about how important the workshop was and how it would help to deliver the firm's "vision". This vision turned out to be to raise their already substantial revenues (and personal incomes) by 30% over two years. There was no more to it than that, no suggestion of any social purpose behind their work and apparently no questioning that whilst to be big and rich was good, bigger and richer was better. Now, these were not bad people and certainly no worse than me (I was taking their money after all) but I was appalled by the narrowness and paucity of their professed sense of purpose. Surely this was not what I (or storytelling) should be supporting in organisations?

I could see both how naïve I had been in accepting the work without first thinking this through and how easily I had let myself be blinded by the prospect of money. I had no right to take the moral high ground - I had been caught by the same "monkey-trap" as the people I had come to work with. I felt ashamed and almost unable to speak.

"Why *monkey-trap*?" asked my colleague when I tried to explain my dilemma to her that evening.

"Well," I said, "I once heard that in parts of India where people still catch monkeys to eat, they put a morsel of food under a hollowed-out half-coconut shell staked to the ground. They make a small hole in the shell, just large enough for the monkey to reach through and grab the bait underneath. The monkey clenches its fist round the food and, overcome by greed, cannot remove its hand. If it refuses to release its prize, the monkey is caught fast, captured and eaten."

I paused.

"I'm asking myself if I should be here at all and what is the intention behind our work? What good can we do inside a system that is so single-minded in the pursuit of wealth?"

We didn't reach any conclusion that evening beyond a decision to hold these questions in mind as we did the workshop. A few days later, I joined a friend, Professor Peter Reason, on his yacht *Coral* at Plymouth for a few days of sailing and soulful conversation.

"So - apart from the money - why do you do this work?" he asked as we sat in the cockpit together in bright sunshine. "It is perfectly clear that the industrial growth society isn't sustainable. Aren't you just propping it up?"

I gripped the tiller and felt myself squirm under his challenging gaze as I attempted an answer. "That's the danger, isn't it? But it has to be about more than that or else it's not worth doing. I think, at its best, there is something about bringing the *life-world* into the *system-world*. If we can get people to relate to each other from a more human and humane place - which storytelling is so good at doing - then surely they will question some of the ways that our institutions operate. I think the storyteller's real work in organisations is essentially subversive: to call into question the unspoken assumptions about power and purpose that drive our institutions, to help people at all levels inside and outside organisations find their voices and speak truth to power. If, as a society, we can do that then maybe - just maybe - we can put the horse before the cart again and our institutions will better serve our human needs instead of ignoring or suppressing them to serve their own purposes."

"Well that's fine and dandy," said Peter. "And you are going to do all this by yourself are you?"

"Of course not," I snapped back, needled by his ironic questioning. "It's huge and even I am not that grandiose. I don't know what can be done - if anything - to turn the tide. I just know that storytelling is what I do and I want to try and do some good with it as and when I get the chance. I want to make a difference and I need to make a living..." My voice trailed off.

"It *is* huge," said Peter gently. "Too big for any of us. We just have to do what we can. My life's work has been about participative research, about the power of collaborating with others for worthwhile ends. I wonder what could be achieved if you got together with other people who feel the same way about storytelling as you do?"

Even for me, an introvert and not a natural collaborator, it seemed obvious that he was right. There was almost nothing I could do alone but maybe it was possible to be a catalyst who would bring together people - storytellers, leaders, researchers, consultants and developers - who shared an interest in the potential of storytelling in organisations to do some good in the world. Together, perhaps, we might create a community of practice and inquiry that would be able to make a difference. It would be a paradoxical enterprise: an attempt to create a liberating structure, an organisation operating in the context of the system world but permeated by the human values and concerns of the life world, inclusive rather than exclusive, inspired by a spirit of generosity and mutual support. Quite a challenge!

My first port of call was my dear friend Sue Hollingsworth, once my teacher at the International School for Storytelling and by now a close colleague. Her eyes lit up at once. "It's a great idea. I'd love to be part of something like that." With her backing I then approached another friend, Margaret Bishop, who was much newer to the world of storytelling and who I knew would offer a different and complementary perspective.

She too readily agreed to help and we three began to hatch a plot.

Our first meeting was at a café in London. It was easy to agree that we needed some sort of event to bring people together and we decided that we would convene a gathering that coming December, still many months away, to give ourselves time to plan and prepare. We talked about storytelling and why we thought that it mattered so much, about how we came to be involved with storytelling and about our hopes for the gathering.

"I want us to create something together that will have a real influence in the field of storytelling in organisations. I want to bring some good people together and take a stand for a responsible and generative approach to storytelling," I said.

"It's all about relationships," said Sue. "We know lots of good people between us that we can invite. I'm really happy to help you get this off the ground but it is your baby, Geoff. You are the one who has to own whatever it is that we create and take it forward."

"I'm very excited and pleased that you asked me to be involved," said Margaret. "I love stories and I'm curious to see what comes of this but I'm not sure what else I can bring to the party."

"What we need to bring us together and to breathe some life into what we are planning is a story," said Sue. "I've been thinking about this and I'm pretty sure I've got one. It's very short. Would you like to hear it?"

We didn't need to be asked twice. Margaret and I sat back in our chairs, coffee in hand, as Sue told us *Water on the Rock*, the story that was to give its name to our first gathering.

A group of bushmen once led some anthropologists to see some rock paintings in the Kalahari Desert. When they arrived the anthropologists could see nothing. Laughing, the bushmen threw water from their gourds onto the sun-bleached surface of the rock and the images burst into life.

"That's it," Margaret and I said, almost as one.

"It's perfect, Sue," I continued. "I love the image of the rock. I want to create something that's durable and substantial, something that lasts."

"And I'm more of an anthropologist, exploring something that is very old but new to me," said Margaret.

Sue laughed. "That's funny, I like to think of myself as the water splashing on the rock and bringing the paintings to life. We seem to be well-matched, don't we?"

We three continued to meet throughout the year, from frosty mornings in Surrey to rainy afternoons in London and sunlit days walking on the beach in Dorset, gradually clarifying and articulating our intentions and piecing together a design for our inaugural gathering that reflected them. By September we were ready to sound the call to action and we sent out thirty letters inviting people to come and throw some *Water on the Rock*. Each invitation began with the text of the story, followed by an explanation of what we had come to call "Narrative Leadership".

On the surface, the rationale for developing the capacity for narrative leadership in organisations is quite straightforward. If, as leaders, managers or change agents we want to get our point of view across effectively, engage people's energy and commitment, inspire others and open their minds to new possibilities, we need to be able to tell a convincing story. As leaders we have to earn the right to ask for people's commitment by standing up and speaking out for what we believe in. Narrative Leadership demands authentic stories told with skill, integrity and vulnerability. It also requires us to develop a deeper understanding of how stories work, to learn to see more clearly the sea of stories in which we swim.

There is also a deeper rationale for working with narrative leadership. We live in a world bombarded by oppressive narratives, subliminal images, disguised messages, and political slogans. It is crucial for our future - especially at this time of urgent environmental, social and ecological challenges - that we develop skill and discernment in telling and listening to leadership narratives. We must learn how to differentiate between narratives that are self-interested and self-serving (and thereby diminishing of others) and those that come from a place of greater mutuality and genuine engagement (and thereby potentially life enhancing).

Our dream is to bring together a group of people - academic researchers, storytellers, leadership development consultants and practitioners, and organisational and other leaders - to co-create a *Centre for Narrative Leadership* in order to develop the practice of narrative leadership. We need to build our understanding of how story can support worthwhile work in the world; to grow and share our expertise; to generate and disseminate useful knowledge; to become a community of inquiry as well as a community of practice; and to establish our presence as leaders in this emerging field.

In the end, twenty four people answered the call and gathered at Charney Manor in Oxfordshire in December 2007 for two extraordinary days of sharing stories, passionate discussions, open-space sessions and talking about the kind of centre that we wanted to create. There was enormous goodwill for the enterprise coupled with a longing for more such gatherings where, as practitioners from many different disciplines and backgrounds across the field, we could periodically meet - like wanderers visiting an oasis - to refresh ourselves, exchange traveller's tales and replenish our storytelling reserves.

In the course of those two days, the form of *Centre for Narrative Leadership* began to emerge. It became clear that we were more interested in building relationships than in creating formal structures; that we wanted to grow organically and by extending personal invitations rather than by formal membership; that we wanted to follow a communitarian path in our association rather than one that was competitive; that we were seeking to build a sustainable community driven by values rather than an organisation driven by profit.

In a quiet way, the Centre has taken root and flourished since that first meeting. We held two more gatherings in 2008 (*Sowing the Seed* in July and *Cathedrals in the Heart* in December) at which participants shared their practice freely with each other in self-organised workshops and another two

(*Apples from Heaven* and *Keys of the Kingdom*) in 2009. At the time of this writing, a further gathering *Today and Tomorrow* is being planned. To date, some seventy-five people have taken part in one or more of these events and another ninety or so have expressed interest in coming along in the future.

Our guiding ethos has also become clear: the Centre stands for the ethical use of stories in support of human flourishing and the sustainability of the human and "more-than-human" world. We uphold a view of story that encompasses using them for practical, down-to-earth business applications whilst also recognising that storytelling is close to the essence of what it means to be human. And we share the belief that respectful listening to each other's stories is fundamental to equitable relationships and a pre-requisite for healthy communities.

Attempting to create something like the *Centre for Narrative Leadership* is a paradoxical endeavour. It has to be able to operate credibly within the *system-world* but avoid becoming subsumed by it - a tricky tightrope to walk. So far, though, our fledgling community seems to have found a good balance between building a community of practice and making a mark on the emerging field of storytelling in organisations without seeking to claim the territory for ourselves. If John Clare were alive today, I hope he would approve.

I have argued in this book that to be storytellers in the modern world challenges us to go beyond being entertainers (pleasant though it is to entertain) and to put ourselves in service of something greater. Through storytelling we can help to heal ourselves and others, enrich our intimate relationships, bring people together in families and communities, assert human values in organisations, and seek to remedy the disenchantment of the world. These are ambitious and demanding aims but surely ones worth striving for and, as George Bernard Shaw[46] wrote, striving in the service of a mighty purpose is the real source of joy and the hallmark of a life well lived:

This is the true joy in life, being used for a purpose recognized by yourself as a mighty one. Being a force of nature instead of a feverish, selfish little clod of ailments and grievances, complaining that the world will not devote itself to making you happy... I want to be thoroughly used up when I die, for the harder I work, the more I live.

Epilogue
Coming Home to Story

Keep Ithaka always in your mind.
Arriving there is what you are destined for.

CP Cavafy

Epilogue
Coming Home to Story

This book began with the account of a dream that caused me to realise that storytelling was my true vocation. Since then I have learned that, for the storyteller, following such a dream demands (in TS Eliot's words) "not less than everything", that doing so will almost inevitably take him to completely unexpected places, and that the journey never ends, for it is the journey itself that matters most.

The storyteller cannot know where the paths he treads will lead, he can only know whether they are "paths with heart" and if so, he can trust them to take him where he needs to go, provided he remains true to his calling. And this conviction accords with the wisdom of the old stories which tell us that when we do not know where we are going, we can only find our way by being true to ourselves. There is a fascinating detail in the closing scenes of *The Furthest Shore* (the iconic story referred to in Chapter 11 *We Band of Brothers*) that makes exactly this point and shows us what is required to take our rightful place in the world.

The king learns that he has been absent so long that his queen is about to marry an imposter - a man "not unlike himself". It is his absolute determination not to be supplanted by this imposter (or we might say his absolute determination to be true to himself) that drives him to trick the three brothers on the heath out of their hat, cloak and boots (a metaphorical device representing the alignment of head, heart and will). With these he is able to gain the help of the North Wind who finally takes him home after years of wandering.

He put on the hat and his mind became crystal clear; he wrapped the cloak around his chest and felt his heart open wide; he pulled on the boots and his will became indomitable. He wished himself back home on the Furthest Shore and as he did so, he rose into the air with the three brothers shaking their fists and cursing at him far below.

Flying high in the air above land and sea he soon saw ahead the white strand of the Furthest Shore and the castle where he had suffered so much and known so much joy. True to his word, the North Wind set him down at the gate and he stood to one side as the wind rattled and shook at the windows and doors. The castle gate opened and out stepped a man, not unlike himself, to see what was happening and the North Wind picked him up and whisked him away so that he never came back - in this story at least. The wind died away and the king of the Furthest Shore, in his traveller's clothes once more, entered the courtyard and climbed the stone stairs to the throne room.

The imposter has gone; the king has stepped into his own life once more. And so, I believe, it is for all of us. Only by living our lives authentically, by being true to our calling, and by following our "paths with heart", can we rightfully claim our own realm (be that storytelling, writing or any other worthwhile creative endeavour). When we take our rightful place it is as though the world recognises us and welcomes us home. This truth is encoded in the story as a return to the beloved and a second (and thereby sacred) marriage - though in our own lives, the choice to be true to ourselves is not encapsulated in a single grand gesture. Instead, we are faced with the choice minute-by-minute and day-by-day: will we show up as ourselves or will we allow the imposter to rule in our place?

His breath caught and his heart quickened as he looked at his queen. He had no words to say and silent tears ran down his cheeks. She looked at his lined face, his grey-streaked hair and beard, and saw the tenderness in his tear-filled eyes. Could this be him? Then something glinted silver in his hair and she reached out and touched the ring she had plaited there so long ago.

"Oh, my dearest man, I hoped and prayed for your return. I waited such a long time for you that I thought you must be dead. You have come back to me and all is well." They fell into each other's arms, hardly believing their good fortune after their long separation.

That evening, the feast that had been prepared was put to good use as they celebrated the true king's return and renewed their marriage vows. After the food and drink came music and dancing, masques and merriment before retiring for the night. And the king and queen of the Furthest Shore lived in love and happiness, ruling wisely and well until the end of their days on earth.

Life for the protagonist of *The Furthest Shore* does not end with his return; when he is finally reunited with his queen after many trials and a long and arduous journey, it begins anew. They have many years ahead of them in which to care for their realm. Perhaps they go on to have children, the story does not say. But in any event, one gets the feeling that the realm will prosper under their stewardship. And just as the king eventually found his way back home to the Furthest Shore, so I feel that after many trials and a long and arduous journey of my own, I have come home to story. This is my realm, this is where I belong - and I too have work to do.

Homecoming, the story tells us, is not an ending but a new beginning in which, reunited with whatever called us to return, what was once impossible yields to our longing. New possibilities spring up, as if from nowhere. So long as we stay true to what's closest to our hearts, we experience a sense of being in the right place at the right time and things seem to happen around us without effort. As mythologist Joseph Campbell once said "Follow your bliss and the universe will open doors for you where there were only walls."

Contrary to what some critics of Campbell claim, he is not advising us to be happy and hope for the best. I think he is saying that only when we are fully committed to kicking out the imposter (when we are absolutely determined to be true to ourselves) can we be sufficiently clear about our intentions and sufficiently receptive to the universe's response to notice the doors of possibility crack open. So the storyteller must learn to trust the apparently serendipitous way one thing leads to another in the world of storytelling and to pay attention to the faint signals that sometimes herald a door opening.

As I come towards the end of writing this book, I get the sense that such a door is opening for me now and through it lies a potential storytelling project that will offer me fresh challenges as a performer and take me down new paths of discovery.

The project stirred into life in an unlikely way, half way round the world when, recently, I went to India for the first time, travelling with a group of UK public service leaders as part of an international leadership programme. We flew to the city of Bangalore, ostensibly to meet local community activists, social entrepreneurs, business leaders and public servants. But I had another (and to me, secretly much more important) reason for going: I was hoping that I would be able to join a local audience sitting at the feet of a Kathak - a traditional Indian storyteller. Perhaps I would even get to hear (if not fully understand) snatches of some epic tale like the *Ramayana* or the *Mahabharata* told in its original language.

But my hopes were soon dashed. I quickly realised that - despite the generosity of our hosts - I had neither the time nor the contacts to arrange such a thing during the few days I would be in India. I resigned myself to the fact that I would almost certainly not meet a storyteller and devoted myself to making the most of the official visits that had already been organised as part of the programme. After dinner on the final evening of the programme, I offered to tell a couple of stories to my fellow participants. We gathered some chairs together in the garden of our hotel under a large tree decorated with strings of tiny electric lights looping between the branches over our heads. The warm night air was humid and thick with the sound of cicadas as I told them a humorous Indian folktale about the tricksterish behaviour of Nandish, a poor village boy who managed to outwit the notorious crook Somendra and give him a good beating into the bargain.

As I chatted with people after the stories, one of them casually mentioned that he was reading a book called *The Storyteller's Tale*. He told me that it had recently been published in India and that he thought I would enjoy it. I was tired and it was getting late but my ears pricked up and I paid close attention. The title intrigued me and I jotted it down on a scrap of paper and tucked the note in my wallet in the hope that I would be able to track down a copy. I had a hunch that it might be important. Maybe I had found my storyteller after all, albeit in a book rather than in person.

When I got back to England, I felt a buzz of excitement as I retrieved the note of the book title and flipped open my laptop. An internet search soon located an Indian bookseller willing to send me a copy. Early one morning a week or two later, a book-sized package tied with string, wrapped in pages from the *Hindustan Times* and postmarked New Delhi arrived on the doorstep: *The Storyteller's Tale* written by Omair Ahmad and published (in English) by Penguin Books India. I took it back to bed with a mug of tea and read it in a single sitting. The tale - of a storyteller dispossessed of his home by bandits and living off his wits - completely gripped me. I relished the playful way that stories were told, transformed and flirtatiously bandied back and forth between the storyteller and the bandit chief's wife in an erotically-charged storytelling "duel". The author seemed to have a deep understanding and appreciation of the storyteller's art and the stories themselves were lively and dramatic. "This would make a fantastic performance piece," I thought.

I decided then and there that I would write to the author to tell him how much I liked *The Storyteller's Tale* and to ask for his blessing for me to use it as the basis of a storytelling performance. Omair replied to my email as soon as it arrived, pleased that I had enjoyed his book ("I mean why write except to tell a story and hope that other people like it?") and gave his full support for my suggestion. At Omair's urging, the publishers also eventually agreed that I could go ahead and give not-for-profit performances based on his book, which will give me the opportunity both to promote the book and raise some money for Indian charities. Apparently without effort on my part, a door had opened; the universe had done its bit. What would happen next, I realised, was up to me.

At the time of writing these words, I am working hard on *The Storyteller's Tale* in preparation for its first performance. Everyone to whom I have turned for help has responded enthusiastically. A friend who plays the *tambour* and sings Indian *ragas* has agreed to join me for the performance, the owner of a suitable venue has offered me its use, and others have volunteered their time to coach me and to direct the performance. I have been invited to perform at the Toronto Storytelling Festival and, taking my courage in both hands, I have accepted. It will be a big step up for me as a performer but I am determined to do justice to the occasion and to serve the story as well as I possibly can. I believe that once having opened the door for me, the universe demands that I not allow some imposter to walk onto the stage.

Soon, I plan to return to India, this time to Delhi to meet the book's author Omair Ahmad, to travel in the landscape in which he has set the story and to spend some time in Jodhpur, where a friend has a *haveli* (courtyard house) in the ancient blue quarter of the city below the mighty citadel of Mehrangarh Fort. There I hope to tell *The Storyteller's Tale* in its native land. I might even meet a real live Indian storyteller this time.

I feel greatly blessed that I have chosen the way of the storyteller (or perhaps that it has chosen me). It has brought me many gifts, as the stories in this book have shown. It has also enabled me to share those gifts with fellow-travellers and it has opened up an endless vista of possibilities. The great beauty of storytelling is that it is open to all. To follow the calling to be a professional storyteller may be a lifetime's work but it is also true that to be human is to tell stories. As they say in India, *"kathaa kahe so kathak"* which can be loosely translated as, "Whoever tells a story is a storyteller." I hope that this book will encourage all who read it to open their hearts, let their imaginations soar and give voice to the story.

Notes

Prologue

1 Barber, A. (1993) *The Mousehole Cat*, Walker Books, London.

Chapter 1

2 Barks, C. (1997) *The Essential Rumi*, Castle Books, New Jersey, pp171-172.
3 Hillman, J. (1983) *Healing Fiction*, Spring, Dallas, pp46-47.
4 Ong, W.J. (2002) *Orality and Literacy*, Routledge, London, p73.

Chapter 2

5 Kornfield, J. and C. Feldman, Eds. (1996). *Soul Food*, HarperSanFrancisco, California.

Chapter 3

6 Lipman, D. (1999) *Improving Your Storytelling: Beyond the Basics for All Who Tell Stories in Work or Play*, August House, pp17-18.

Chapter 5

7 Bly, R. (1991) *The Light Around the Body*, Harper and Row, New York.
8 Frank, A.W. (1997). *The Wounded Storyteller*, University of Chicago Press, Chicago, p57.
9 Ibid p18.

Chapter 6

10 Twelve men and eight women, our ages ranged from early 30s to mid 50s. We came from an interesting and quite diverse range of national and ethnic backgrounds: 11 English, 3 Welsh, 1 American, 1 Canadian, 1 Greek, 1 Australian, 1 Punjabi, 1 West Indian.

11 Bakan, D. (1966) *The Duality of Human Existence: Isolation and Communion in Western Man*, Beacon Press, Boston, pp 14-15.

12 Bruner, J. (1986) *Actual Minds, Possible Worlds*, Harvard University Press, Cambridge, Mass. and Bruner, J. (1990) *Acts of Meaning*, Harvard University Press, Cambridge, Mass.

13 Polkinghorne, D. (1988) *Narrative Knowing and the Social Sciences*, SUNY Press, Albany, p150.

14 Randall, W. L. (1995) *The Stories We Are: An Essay on Self-Creation*, University of Toronto Press, Toronto.

15 Dunne, J.S. (1973) *Time and Myth: A Meditation on Storytelling as an Exploration of Life and Death*, University of Notre Dame Press, Notre Dame.

Chapter 7

16 Berman, M. (2005) *The Shaman and The Storyteller*, Superscript, Newtown, p60.

17 Quoted from Rachel's MSc dissertation, pseudonymously and with her permission.

18 Quoted from email correspondence with Carrie, pseudonymously and with her permission.

19 Ong, W.J. (1982) *Orality and Literacy*, Routledge, London pp 31-57.

20 Polster, E. (1990) *Every Person's Life is Worth a Novel*, Norton, New York.

Chapter 8

21 Moss, R. (1998) *Dreamgates*, Three Rivers Press, New York, p144.

22 Adapted from *Tales from the Norse*, (originally collected by Asbjørnsen and Moe, translated by Sir George Webbe Dasent), published by Blackie and Sons Ltd, Glasgow, undated (late nineteenth century).

23 The names of participants have been changed, when so requested, to maintain anonymity.

Chapter 9

24 Frank, A.W. (1997). *The Wounded Storyteller*, University of Chicago Press, Chicago, p23.

25 Written and composed by William Witherspoon, Paul Riser and James Dean; originally released on Motown Records in 1966, sung by Jimmy Ruffin.

Chapter 10

26 The version that we learned and which is quoted here comes from Burrows, A. and J. Macy (2005) *In Praise of Mortality: Selections from Rainer Maria Rilke's Duino Elegies and Sonnets to Orpheus*, Riverhead Books, New York.

27 Grace's account is included with her permission, though 'Grace' is a pseudonym, as is 'Jane' who was referred to earlier in my account.

28 For example White, M and D. Epston (1990) *Narrative Means to Therapeutic Ends*, Norton, New York.

29 For example Gersie, A. (1997) *Reflections on Therapeutic Storymaking*, Jessica Kingsley Publishers, London.

30 Visit www.biographywork.org for more about the work of the Biography and Social Development Trust or see, for example, Schöttelndreier, J. (1990) *Life Patterns: Responding to Life's Questions, Crises and Challenges*, Hawthorn Press, Stroud.

Chapter 11

31 There are some excellent books exploring the nature of women's stories. Perhaps the best known is *Women Who Run With the Wolves* by Jungian analyst and storyteller Clarissa Pinkola Estés (published by Ballantine Books, New York in 1992). Allan B Chinen's *Waking the World: Tales of Women and the Heroic Feminine* (published by Tarcher Putnam, New York in 1997) has more to say on the subject. I would also recommend Erica Helm Meade's *Tell It by Heart: Women and the Healing Power of Story* (published by Open Court, Chicago in 1995) and Kathleen Ragan's *Fearless Girls, Wise Women and Beloved Sisters:*

Heroines in Folktales from Around the World (published by WW Norton, New York in 1998).

32 Bly, R. (1990) *Iron John: A Book About Men*, Addison-Wesley, New York.

33 Meade, M. (1994) *Men and the Water of Life: Initiation and the Tempering of Men*, HarperSanFrancisco, San Francisco.

34 Campbell, J. (1968) *The Hero with a Thousand Faces*, Princeton University Press, Princeton. p30.

35 Chinen, A.B. (1994) *Beyond the Hero: Classic Stories of Men in Search of Soul*, Tarcher Putnam, New York.

36 *Rites of Passage* run by the Mandorla team at Cae Mabon.

Chapter 12

37 Freefall writing is a technique invented by Canadian W.O. Mitchell and developed by Barbara Turner-Vesselago who teaches it in fabulous workshops around the world. It encourages a free and unedited flow of creative writing. If you ever have a chance to go to one, even half a chance, then go!

Chapter 14

38 For a scholarly exploration of these themes, see Berman, M. (1981) *The Reenchantment of the World*, Cornell University Press, Ithaca, New York.

39 Downloaded from the website of the *Alliance for Wild Ethics* on 21st January 2011 http://www.wildethics.org/home.html.

40 Macy, J. *Twelve Guidelines for Action in the World* downloaded 12th April 2011 from http://www.joannamacy.net/livingsystems/the-holonic-shift.html.

41 Christmas in all its Catholic, Protestant, Coptic and Orthodox variations, Hanukkah in the Jewish tradition, Diwali for Hindus, Sikhs, Jains and Buddhists, Saturnalia for the ancient Romans, Yuletide and the Midwinter Solstice for Pagans - the list is almost endless.

42 About the same time, in the fourth century BCE, the great 15,000 seat, open-air theatre at Epidaurus, in the Peloponnese, was established close to the Asklepieion

- the most widely-known healing sanctuary of the day. Apparently a trip to the theatre was frequently prescribed as part of a patient's treatment!

Chapter 15

43 Habermas, J. (1987). *The Theory of Communicative Action (Lifeworld and System: A Critique of Functionalist Reason: Volume 2)*, Beacon Press, Uckfield, pp381-383.
44 See *Chapter 4: A Moment of Grace* for more about this story.
45 Similar processes have been used in many parts of the world. Wikipedia lists 20 instances http://en.wikipedia.org/wiki/Truth_and_reconciliation_commission (retrieved 29 Jan 2011).

Chapter 16

46 Shaw, G.B. (2004) *Man and Superman (Epistle Dedicatory)*, Penguin, London.

Acknowledgements

This book has been a long time in the making and at least three years in the writing, during which time I have received inspiration, encouragement and support from more sources than I could possibly mention or even call to mind. But there are some people without whose contributions it simply would not exist and I am enormously grateful to them in myriad ways.

Bernard Kelly told the first traditional story I ever heard (The Banyan Deer) so brilliantly that I fell in love with storytelling on the spot. Ashley Ramsden, Sue Hollingsworth and Roi Gal-Or generously shared their deep knowledge of the craft of storytelling with me and several generations of apprentices. My friend Richard Olivier challenged me a decade or more ago to find the project that would become the rest of my life, and has encouraged me ever since to believe in myself as a writer and storyteller. Debra Baptiste and Dan Yashinsky took a leap of faith and invited me to perform at the Toronto Storytelling Festival which has led to many other opportunities.

When it came to writing the book I was fortunate to have discovered writing teacher, mentor and editor nonpareil Barbara Turner-Vesselago who always insisted on the best that I could do. Sarah Bird of Vala Publishing Co-operative has been a true ally and I am both delighted and honoured that *Coming Home to Story* will be the first of what I hope will be many Vala publications.

My partner Chris Seeley has consistently championed my own creative journey. The typography and graphic images that grace these pages are her most visible contribution to this book, but she has also joined me in many storytelling performances and has always refused to let me find reasons not to write. For these things and for many others which have immeasurably enriched my life I thank her sincerely.

About the author

Born into the post-war baby-boomer generation, Geoff Mead was the first member of his family to go to university (and the first to drop out). He quickly returned to complete his studies in mediaeval history after a salutary period washing cars for a living. With not much idea of what he really wanted to do, he cut off his shoulder-length hair and joined the police service which he left three decades later as a chief superintendent.

During those years he did pretty much everything from walking the beat to directing national police leadership programmes, and from commanding a police district to training with the FBI in Virginia, USA. En route he also found time to complete an MBA, a postgraduate diploma in Gestalt psychology and a PhD in action research. In his fifties, life took a different turn when he discovered the magic of stories and began to explore their power to liberate the human spirit. Now, he performs traditional stories, runs story-based workshops, and teaches storytelling at venues in the UK and as far afield as Spain, Canada and Japan.

As an organisational consultant, keynote speaker and workshop leader, he has taken his work on "narrative leadership" into the boardrooms of blue-chip companies, universities and government departments. He is on the faculty of the Cabinet Office's Top Management Programme and is a visiting research fellow at the University of Bath. In 2007, he co-founded the Centre for Narrative Leadership (www.narrativeleadership.org) a not-for-profit network dedicated to developing the field of storytelling in organisations.

He has four grown up children, five grandchildren and an entirely unreasonable love of Morgan sports cars. He divides his time between his partner's house in the Cotswolds and Lyme Regis where he lives and writes in sight of the sea.

About Vala

Vala is an **adventure**
in **community supported** publishing.

We are a **co-operative**
bringing books to the world that **explore** and **celebrate**
the human spirit with **brave** and **authentic**
ways of thinking and being.

Books that seek to help us find our own **meanings**
that may lead us in **new** and *unexpected* directions.

Vala's co-operative members
- suggest authors
- design
- write
- support the writing process
- get together for book-making evenings
- promote and sell Vala books through their own
networks.

Members come together to **celebrate** and **launch** each
new publication. Together we decide what happens to any
profit that we make.

Vala exists to bring us all into fuller relationship with our
world, ourselves, and each other.

To find out more visit us at *www.valapublishers.coop*

 Vala